DON'T SWEAT THE SMALL STUFF IN LOVE

DON'T SWEAT
THE SMALL STUFF
IN LOVE

Simple Ways to Nurture and Strengthen
Your Relationships While Avoiding the Habits That
Break Down Your Loving Connection

RICHARD CARLSON, Ph.D., AND KRISTINE CARLSON

New York

Library of Congress Cataloging-in-Publication Data

Carlson, Richard.
Don't sweat the small stuff in love : simple ways to nurture and
strengthen your relationships while avoiding the habits that break
down your loving connection / by Richard and Kristine Carlson.
p.   cm.
ISBN 0-7868-6509-1
1. Love.   2. Man-woman relationships.   I. Carlson, Kristine.
II. Title.   III. Title: Do not sweat the small stuff in love.
BF575.L8C24 1999
306.7—dc21   99-27271
                                                CIP

First Edition

10 9 8 7 6 5 4 3 2 1

BOOK DESIGN BY JENNIFER ANN DADDIO

We dedicate this book to our daughters, Jazzy and Kenna.
The greatest gift we can give you is the love
we have for each other.

ACKNOWLEDGMENTS

First and foremost, we would like to send a special and heartfelt thanks to our parents—Pat and Ted Anderson and Barbara and Don Carlson—for being the special people they are. We love you all so very much. Thank you for teaching us, sharing your love and ideas with us, and for raising us to be happy people.

Thanks also to Jazzy and Kenna for bringing so much joy and laughter to our lives. You are loved now and forever.

We would also like to acknowledge our editor, Leslie Wells, for her magical skill with words and the entire staff at Hyperion for being so much fun to work with. As always, a special thanks to Patti Breitman for being a wonderful agent and, more importantly, a trusted and valued friend. Thanks also to Linda Michaels for sharing this book with people all over the world.

And finally, a sincere thanks to you, our readers. We hope so much that your relationships will be strengthened and nourished by reading this book.

CONTENTS

DON'T SWEAT THE SMALL STUFF IN LOVE

INTRODUCTION

When you ask people questions like, "How is your relationship going," you will often hear replies like, "It's okay, I guess," or a variety of other equally unenthusiastic or unsure responses. For whatever reasons, many people seem to believe that it's normal and perfectly acceptable to settle for an "okay" relationship. Sometimes, even couples who report that they have a good relationship appear to be confused about what a "good" relationship really means. In other words, they might say they have a nice relationship, yet they seem to experience or express ongoing irritation and frustration with their partner, or with at least some aspects of their relationship. There may be ongoing conflict or bickering, a lack of harmony or satisfaction, resentment, a desire for their partner to be different, or simply a shortage of true joy and gratitude.

We're going to ask you to consider that whatever shape your relationship is in—from troubled to absolutely wonderful—it can be even better, with very little effort. While no relationship is perfect, and every relationship is unique, we believe that any partnership, romantic or otherwise, can be improved by implementing some very simple strategies designed to lighten your spirits, open your heart, enhance your life, and broaden your perspective. That's what this book is all about.

Human beings are remarkable creatures in the sense that when we have a specific vision or goal, we are often able to achieve that goal, or at the very least approach it. In terms of your relationships, this means that it's important that you have the highest vision possible. It suggests that you can have it all: You can be best friends, soulmates, and true partners, in every sense of the word. Individually and as a couple, you can become more loving, lighthearted, peaceful, generous, grateful, patient, accepting, and forgiving. You can also develop greater perspective, a better sense of humor, better listening skills, and perhaps most importantly, the ability to take yourself a little less seriously. It's possible for you to have more of all of these things and, for that matter, any other virtuous qualities that you deem important. And perhaps the best part of all is that when you or your partner falls short, you'll be easy on yourself, and on your relationship—you won't "sweat it." All it takes is intention and a bit of practice.

Despite our optimistic natures, we're not unrealistic. We're not suggesting that if you stop sweating the small stuff in love, you will be without problems or issues, or that you won't become crabby with one another, at least every once in a while. Nor are we suggesting that there won't be times when you'll experience doubt or even times when you think your partner is going to drive you crazy. We are suggesting, however, that whatever frustration you do experience will be lessened and that even your struggles and troubles can be approached with greater ease and perspective. In other words, even in the midst of a problem, you will have the confidence to know that you can rise above that problem and solve it, and while you're at it, get back to your loving connection.

Writing this book together has been enormous fun and has been one of the highlights of our lives together. It's given us an opportunity to carefully reflect on what we believe to be the keys to a loving and nurturing connection. While neither of us necessarily considers ourselves to be an expert on relationships, we do feel that we have a darn good one. We've been married for fourteen years and have known one another for seventeen. A vast majority of the time we've been loving, kind, and respectful of one another, and we do consider ourselves to be the best of friends. While, on occasion, we can get on each other's nerves, we're happy to say that it's extremely rare.

As we reflect on our own relationship, it's clear to us that while we both have many flaws, our greatest strength is that we don't sweat the small stuff—very often. Most of the time we're able to take each other in stride and focus on strengths instead of weaknesses. More often than not, we let things go instead of holding them against each other. Both of us are more committed to being kind than to being right, and each of us has the ability to laugh at ourselves. We've found that when we're not too uptight, life gets a whole lot easier and we experience a great deal more love.

Obviously, there are many enormous challenges in life and in all relationships. And, unfortunately, pain is a reality for every one of us during certain times in our lives. It's fascinating, however, to examine the way most people handle the truly "big stuff." You'll probably agree that, for the most part, people handle the serious parts of life with courage, dignity, and creativity. When a family has a sick child, for example, everyone comes together. There is sharing, support, prayers, strength, and acts of selfless love. Likewise, when a couple experiences a tragedy—a sickness or death in the family, bankruptcy, or some other painful or difficult event—there is often a coming together, joint strength, sacrifice, creative ideas, and stamina.

Luckily, however, most of life doesn't consist of the really big stuff. In other words, the good news is, we're not fired from a job every day, nor do we file for divorce or have to run to the emergency room every few hours. These things do happen and when they do, they can be devastating. However, this kind of event tends to be occasional and spread out. In a weird way, it's almost as though we're more equipped to deal with the big things than we are the smaller stuff. We know we must get through them, so we bring out the best in ourselves and in each other.

The truth, of course, is that a vast majority of our lives is consumed with the day-to-day, moment-to-moment small stuff—dealing with each other and our daily lives, minor hassles and frustrations, traffic, unreturned phone calls, more hassles, chaos, messes, disagreements, responsibilities, lost items, noise, and so forth. It's for this reason that we believe it's so important to learn to deal with the small stuff—it's in our face, all the time. We've even found that as we've learned to deal with the small stuff with more equanimity, we've handled the bigger things that come along a bit better as well.

Our hope is that the strategies in this book will help you deal with the small aggravations in your relationships with more ease and perspective. We think you'll find that as you let go of the distractions of the small stuff, you'll find new, effortless ways to nurture and love one another.

A note about the way this was written: We collaborated on the entire book, but some of the strategies were written more from Richard's point of view, and some from Kris's. For simplicity's sake, those that were written from Kris's point of view are marked "(Kris)" after the strategy's title. Those from Richard's point of view, or from both our points of view, are unmarked.

Our goal is not to have you model our relationship or to paint a picture of how you ought to be. Rather, our hope is that the ideas in this book will help you to create the relationships of your own dreams. So, as we begin our adventure together, our initial advice is this: Shoot for the stars. The higher your vision, the higher you'll climb. And what's more, you'll stop sweating the small stuff—or at least most of it! As this begins to happen, you'll experience more enthusiasm and love than you might have imagined to be possible. Good luck and have fun.

—Richard and Kris Carlson

1.

MOSTLY, BE PALS

I had to choose a single characteristic that has made our relationship remain special, fun, and vibrant over the years, it would probably be that the two of us are, first and foremost, really good pals. Make no mistake about it—we're all the other things too. We are committed to each other and faithful. We share an overwhelming love for our children, similar values and goals, many of the same friends, shared interests, and mutual respect, as well as an attraction for one another. We are also blessed with the same spiritual values and beliefs. Yet, as wonderful and important as all of these other characteristics are, none of them guarantees keeping your love for each other alive and strong.

After all, there are many faithful couples who bicker in the car on their way to church. There are plenty of wonderful and dedicated parents who share similar values. Yet, they are constantly irritated at one another. There are also tons of couples who have mutual friends, share similar hobbies and interests, and are physically attracted to each other, who nevertheless fight like crazy, experience jealousy, and just can't seem to get along for extended periods of time.

When you are good friends first, however, everything seems to take care of itself. Pals support one another. They are patient and kind, and make allowances for each other's imperfections. Friends are excellent communicators, and usually very good listeners. While they can also be serious, when appropriate, pals also find it easy to have fun, and to laugh. They stay connected, sharing in the good times and being there for each other during difficult times.

The best way to remain (or get back to being) pals is to see what's in it for you and for your relationship. Once you are convinced that having a great friendship is the best way to secure a great relationship, the rest is pretty easy. Keep reminding yourself that your goal is to treat your partner with the same kindness, appreciation, and respect as you would your very best friend in the world. When in doubt, ask yourself, "If this person were my best friend, how would I respond and how would I act?"

Many people say, "My partner *is* my best friend," but most don't actually back up that statement with thoughts, feelings, and actions consistent with it. To the contrary, many individuals treat their partner with more jealousy, expectations, and demands—and with less appreciation, respect, and sensitivity—than they would a friend. Many people treat their partner as if they own them, and seem more interested in the image of who they want their partner to be than in who their partner really is.

If a friend said to you, "My dream is to change careers. It will mean less money, but I know I'll be happier," or if she said, "My dream is to live near the ocean," you'd probably be enthused and supportive. But what if your partner said the same thing to you? How would you respond? Would you be supportive, take it to heart, and try to help her make it happen? Or would you automatically disregard it, or in some way minimize it—saying or thinking, "You can't (or shouldn't) do that. It's not practical. It's not what I want."

Obviously, the spirit of your answer is what's most important. It's not always possible, practical, or even desirable for your partner to do everything he or she wants to do. You can't always move or change jobs. We're not suggesting that it's necessary to always want what your partner wants, or that it's your responsibility to make it happen. Instead, we are saying that it's important to remember how friends treat friends and to take that into consideration in your relationship. What's most important is that your partner knows that you're genuinely supportive of her dreams, whether she can fulfill them or not.

We can assure you, firsthand, that being really good friends is a gift, and a goal worth pursuing. When you are good pals, you somehow find a way to meet in the middle, and to share in each other's dreams without feeling like you're sacrificing a thing. Implementing this strategy may take some reflection and the willingness to change a few habits, but it's well worth the effort.

2.

LEARN TO LAUGH
AT YOURSELF

Almost nothing immunizes you from day-to-day frustration more than a healthy sense of humor—particularly the ability to laugh at yourself. Every long-term relationship gets to a point where your partner knows you almost as well as you know yourself. He will see your quirks, anticipate your unhealthy responses, and know the ways that you sometimes get in your own way. Even if you tried, it would be difficult to hide your true self from your partner.

If you are unable to laugh at yourself, you're in for a long, bumpy ride. You will struggle in your relationships because, as your partner teases you, notices your flaws, and occasionally points them out, you will feel and probably act a bit defensive. This, in turn, will exacerbate and highlight your weaknesses, making them seem far more significant. What's more, your reactions to your partner's comments will create additional issues for the two of you to deal with, and your "small stuff" will start to seem like big stuff.

If you look around at the happiest and most loving relationships, you'll almost always notice that both people have an ability to laugh at themselves. Both partners will have the perspective necessary to stay lighthearted as their own imperfections come to the surface. This creates an environment where occasional teasing or kidding around is okay, and where one feels safe in making observations or suggestions. Your relationship has the chance to deepen and grow because both parties feel safe.

It's quite remarkable to observe what happens to a potentially heated interaction when someone is able to keep their sense of humor. In most cases, the situation is diffused and simply melts away. For example, we were sharing time with another couple when the woman made a slightly snide comment to her husband. Specifically, she said, "You talk too much." His response speaks to the point of this strategy. He laughed to himself and said, very gently, "You're right, I sure can dominate a conversation." More than his words, his ability to see a grain of truth in his wife's statement, to remain humble, and to be willing to chuckle at his own tendency resolved the situation before it had a chance to gain any momentum. Often, when you keep your sense of humor and remain humble, your partner will sense when he has been too harsh and will end up apologizing for his comment. Even if this doesn't happen, it doesn't really matter because to you, it was no big deal to begin with.

Over the years, we've seen hundreds of similar conversations turn ugly because, instead of keeping a sense of humor and remaining lighthearted, the person on the receiving end of the not-so-nice comment became defensive and took himself too seriously. His inability to have a sense of humor encouraged him to lash back, argue, or start a fight.

When someone takes himself too seriously, you can sense it, even when he keeps his reactions to himself. His mood changes, as do his mannerisms, his tone of voice, and his body language. There are no two ways about it: Without a sense of humor, you end up suffering.

Remember that, as wonderful as you are, your partner spends a great deal of time with you. If he or she makes occasional observations that are less than sugar-coated, there may be a grain of truth in what they are saying. But even if they are off base entirely, it's probably in your best interest to simply let it go—laugh it off. By laughing at yourself, not taking yourself so seriously, you will become much easier to be around. Your partner won't feel as though she has to walk around on eggshells, making sure you don't get upset. And in the end, because you will have created a more nourishing and safe environment for your partner, your relationship will be more loving and a heck of lot more fun.

3.

LET IT GO ALREADY

One day I was driving in a car, listening to a radio call-in talk show. In less than half an hour, three people called in to complain about something their spouse had done, or in one case "may have done." In all three cases, the so-called issue had happened at least a year prior to the call. One woman's issue was that her husband "may have flirted" with another woman some two years ago. She was absolutely consumed with this, unable to let it go, and was wondering what to do. Another complained that, in years past, her husband had seemed distant and had become a poor listener. She was trying to figure out what she had done wrong. It was as if she were playing Ping-Pong in her mind, saying things like, "It could have been this or it may have been that." Finally, a man called to share his frustration that in their first year of marriage, his new wife had racked up some hefty credit card bills. He couldn't sleep nights because he was caught up in the fear that she might, at some point, repeat this behavior, despite the fact that she seemed to have curbed her habit and learned her lesson. He was still angry with her for "what she had done to their future security."

I felt like yelling, "Let it go already!" But that was hardly the advice the hostess was offering. To the contrary, she encouraged them to get even more caught up and analytical about the events and issues, and to fill their heads with doubts, fears, and additional concerns. She would say things like,

"Have you considered that there may be a pattern here?" and "Oh my God, I've heard this before. Be careful."

Before I go on, let me assure you that I'm not making a case for flirting outside of marriage, poor listening skills, or overspending. All three issues can, and often do, contribute to problems in marriages, as well as other relationships. However, most people seem to completely ignore the negative impact of hanging on to such issues to a point of diminishing return—and the impact this unwillingness to let things go has on our relationships. We forget what a drag it is to be around people who can't let go of things and who hold on to past issues. We fail to realize how difficult it is to remain loving to someone who holds us to unrealistic expectations, and who makes no room in their heart for the fact that we are human. There's an old saying that applies not only to these three callers, but to most of the rest of us as well: "Enough is enough."

Relationships can be challenging enough without the added burden of keeping past issues alive and vibrant in your mind. It's helpful to remind yourself of what happens to your own capacity to love, forgive, and grow when you are consumed with something that is over and done with. Usually, when your head is filled with concerns, reminders of past issues, and problems, you are filled with fear, suspicion, and frustration—practically anything but love. Your frustration will usually spill over into other areas as well, and you'll probably end up being upset about all sorts of "small stuff."

We're not talking about burying your head in the sand. The truth is, we all make mistakes, act less than perfect, and have at least occasional errors in judgment. The ideal environment to get through these things, however, is an environment of forgiveness and nonjudgment. In other words, if someone you love has made any type of mistake, the best you can do is remain loving and supportive yourself, and not turn the issue into a gigantic event. That way, your rapport will remain intact and your partner will feel comfortable discussing the issues between you and will feel supported in your growth as a couple.

So, if you're carrying around or still holding on to issues from your past, it may be time to simply let them go. Instead of harboring negative feelings and staying uptight, make the decision to forgive, forget, and move on. You'll be rewarded with a richer, more open and honest, and far more loving and nourishing relationship.

4.

TURN UP THE HEAT

♥ In theory, if your home was too cold, there would be two primary ways to create a warmer temperature. The first would be to shore up the cracks. You'd walk around the house making sure the windows were tightly closed; you'd check the weather-stripping, the insulation in the attic, and any cracks in the walls, around the edges of doors, and so forth. In doing so, you'd keep additional outside cold air from entering the house. The other, more direct (and much quicker) approach would be to simply turn up the heat. Bingo—in a matter of a few minutes, your home would be warm and cozy—irrespective of any tiny cracks.

You can easily extend this metaphor to your relationship. You can attempt to create warmth and closeness by fixing everything that's wrong. Theoretically, if you were able to mend each issue and repair every imperfection, you'd have one terrific relationship filled with warmth and love.

But like heating a home, a more direct (and more effective) approach would be to (metaphorically) turn up the heat. In a practical sense, this means that you ignite every warmth indicator you can possibly think of. You become kinder and more generous, and you start dishing out more compliments. You become less critical, stubborn, and judgmental. Instead of being irritated, you practice patience and forgiveness. You begin to use more eye contact and better listening skills. You choose being kind over being right, and you put the needs of your partner before your own. You say and do the things that you used to say and do when you first met. In short, you do anything and everything that is associated with loving behavior. If you turn up the heat in this way, your relationship will blossom despite the fact that there are tiny flaws. In fact, with enough warmth, most flaws and imperfections will work themselves out without much involvement or effort.

As obvious as this is (when you actually sit down and think about it), it's almost never done. Most of the time the other approach is taken—trying to fix deficiencies. Frequently, people will say, "I can't turn up the heat until certain conditions are met, until he or she begins to change." The problem is, the type of change you're looking for is almost impossible in the absence of enough heat. It's putting the cart before the horse.

Caitlin was frustrated and a little bitter at her husband Fred for his lack of drive since he had been fired from his job. She told me, "I'm sick of his laziness. All he does is sit around. He's not even trying." She further told me that she had no intention of being loving until he got his act together.

I introduced her to the notion of turning up the heat. It took some getting used to, but eventually she agreed that, in principle, it sounded like a good idea. She made some subtle changes and became softer. In her words, she "got off his back." She sat closer to him while they watched TV, and she dropped the heaviness from the issue. She started acting like a friend, someone who cared.

She reported to me that the changes in Fred and in their relationship were remarkable. Fred's spirits began to rise and his sense of humor returned. He was able to open up and share his feelings. Caitlin saw a side to Fred she had never seen before—a more sensitive side.

Within a relatively short period of time, Fred was back on his feet and their relationship was stronger than before Fred had been fired.

The same dynamic applies to any relationship, regardless of what the circumstances might be and whatever challenges you're facing. I've yet to see an instance where becoming more loving wasn't an idea worth considering. See if you can think of some ways you can turn up the heat—you'll be glad you did.

5.

CONSIDER THAT THE GRASS PROBABLY *ISN'T* GREENER

We live in what might be called the "trade-up" era. We trade smaller homes for bigger ones, older cars for newer. We want better jobs, more income, a bigger retirement plan, and better experiences. We want better bodies and to belong to the best gym. It seems that everyone wants a better computer, one that's faster and that can do more things. After all, they are obsolete after a year or two. Popular mottos include "New and Improved" and "Out with the old and in with the new." If you believe the ads, you might even imagine that the best solution to being overextended financially is to get an even bigger loan. That way, you can consolidate your debt and, at the same time, buy more things, different things that are better than what you already have. We want, we want, we want. Always more. Something else is always going to be better.

In a way, it's no wonder that we transfer at least part of this neurotic tendency to our partner. After all, the "something else would be better" philosophy is ingrained into our way of thinking. Why would our relationship be the one exception to this rule? It seems inevitable that we would think of our partner in these same terms, at least once in a while. Maybe someone else would be better looking or a better lover. Or, perhaps they would treat us better or be a better listener or be more attentive. Maybe, with a different partner, our needs would be met more often and we'd finally be satisfied.

This idea is certainly reinforced on television. It seems that almost everyone is either having an affair or finding a new love. No one is satisfied for long.

Obviously there are times when a new partner could be the answer, but this is clearly the exception rather than the norm. And while you may not be in the market or actively looking for a new partner, it's nevertheless important to know that there's a way that even thinking in those terms prevents you from fully enjoying what you already have and from making your relationship all that it can be. When your focus is on what would be better, or on comparing what you have (or who you have) to the fantasy of something (or someone) else, it encourages a great deal of dissatisfaction and frustration.

It's helpful to realize and admit that, often, the fantasy of something different is a lot better than the reality of something different. We've met men and women who have left their spouses for someone else—someone younger or better looking, or someone who gave them more attention or who had more money—or whatever. Without exception, the fantasy was better than the reality. New people may be wonderful, but, like the rest of us, they too have issues. Along with new partners come a new set of problems. Many people say, "If I were with someone else, I wouldn't have to put up with this." That may be true, but you'd have to put up with something else. Guaranteed. There's just no way around it.

This strategy is very helpful if you want to feel more peace and satisfaction in your relationship. It's also quite easy to implement. All you have to do is become aware of the tendency to think that someone else would be better—and keep it in check. That's it—no big deal. And when you find yourself thinking in these terms, try something a little different. Instead of distracting yourself with thoughts of what or who would be better, see if you can find a way to make the relationship you're already in be as good as it can be. Appreciate what you have now and you'll probably discover that the grass isn't always greener.

6.

THROW AWAY
YOUR SCORECARD

♥ If you wanted an absolutely predictable, completely reliable way to guarantee ongoing frustration—and a virtually guaranteed way to adversely affect your relationship—it would be to keep score of what you do, and of what your partner isn't doing. And if you really wanted to compound the problem, you could let your partner know, on a regular basis, how he or she isn't meeting your expectations—and how much more you are doing than they are!

As ludicrous as this idea may seem, it's precisely what many couples do, without knowing it, every day of their lives together. This habit contributes to resentment, frustration, apathy, and an overall breakdown of an otherwise positive relationship.

For various reasons, it's tempting to keep track, either silently or even out loud, of all that you're doing to contribute to the relationship, to make your partner's life easier, and how much you sacrifice in the name of the relationship. You think of how many times in a row you've cleaned the house, or paid the bills, or driven to work, or done the laundry, or bathed the children, or whatever.

Perhaps we do this for fear we won't be appreciated—or maybe it's because we're slightly resentful of the role we find ourselves in—or perhaps it's something altogether different. Whatever the reason, it backfires.

When you engage in this extremely common habit, two things are certain. First, your excessive thinking about the perceived inequities in your relationship will frustrate you and stress you out. When you constantly remind yourself of your own hard work, you'll invariably feel angry at your partner, and in many cases, your loving feelings will diminish. The connection between your thinking and the way you feel is undeniable. As you think about your resentments and fill your mind with your unfair task load, you'll feel the effects of those burdensome thoughts—you'll feel taken advantage of and burned out.

Second, your partner will feel your resentment and built-up tension—which will give him or her more negativity to latch on to and think about. No one wants to feel as though their partner is put off and angered by the contributions they are making. In fact, the usual response to discovering this is to become defensive about how much he or she is doing in comparison. Both parties dig in and think even more about how much they are doing—score cards are flying! Negative feelings surround your relationship, and both partners think the other is to blame.

As your scorecard enters your mind, see if you can drop those thoughts and bring yourself back to a loving feeling. Remind yourself that it's easier to see your own contribution and to take your partner's efforts for granted. For the moment, reverse this thought process. Think not of what your partner *isn't* doing, but instead think of what he is doing. You may discover that some portion of your frustration isn't reality, but simply a mental habit that has crept into your thinking. Each time you dismiss your "this isn't fair" thinking, you'll be contributing to the good will of your relationship. In fact, Kris and I have discovered that, ultimately, keeping your scorecard thinking to a minimum actually contributes more to a loving relationship than any of the more concrete contributions you are making—the ones you are fretting about.

Even if your scorecard mentality persists, and you're absolutely convinced that you are getting the short end of the stick, it's still best that you keep your thinking in check. In doing so, you'll keep your loving feelings alive. Remember, it's always easier to have heartfelt discussions or discuss difficult issues when your heart is filled with love and patience. Admittedly, both Kris and I still occasionally fall into this trap, but luckily it's pretty rare. We think you'll find that if you can nip this tendency in the bud, the mutual love and respect in your relationship will return—or get even stronger.

7

BE KIND FIRST
(KRIS)

Above all else, adopt an attitude of kindness. Make it your highest priority to practice it every day. Start at home—in your relationship. Kindness is one of the primary ingredients in nourishing a warm feeling between two people. In fact, it can be the centerpiece of your entire relationship. It does everything from keeping you close and connected when all is well, to keeping arguments from turning into fights.

Being genuinely kind is not about smiling when you don't feel like it or acting cheerful when you're low. Rather, it's about treating your partner (and everyone else) the way you would like to be treated. It's been said many times that, in life, we teach people how to treat us. It's certainly true that the best way to teach others (including our partner) that we would like to be treated with kindness is by offering our kindness first. Indeed, kindness is extremely contagious.

Sue, married for twenty-five years, always speaks about her husband, Rick, with a smile in her eyes that makes you feel as though they must be happy together. I asked her what she felt was the key ingredient to the obvious success and happiness of her marriage. Without even having to think about it, she said it was because she is married to one of the "kindest people imaginable."

For example, Sue said that she has a tendency to be stubborn about her ideas. During a stubborn moment, Rick's ability to stay calm and kind tends to diffuse Sue's rigidity. Rather than becoming a power struggle, his kindness helps both of them keep their perspective. Or, on a bad day, Sue might come home tired and irritable. Rather than reacting to her mood, Rick simply gives her some space, allowing her to work through her feelings in her own time. He's always there if she needs him, but doesn't bombard her with questions or suggestions.

It's important to treat your partner with the same kindness that you would give your very best friend. You start with the little things—listening from the heart and being respectful and thoughtful. Being kind means asking permission, when appropriate, and saying "I'm sorry" when you're wrong or when you make a mistake. Being kind means being polite. It also involves trying to anticipate the needs of your partner and asking yourself, "What would make him happy right now—is there anything I can do?" Kindness really is about the simple things.

I'm biased, of course, but I live with one of the kindest people on this planet. Richard wakes up almost every day with a smile in his eyes and a true appreciation for life. He responds to even my worst PMS days with gentleness and understanding. Because of this, it's hard for me to become overly angry with him over little things like his tendency to rumple his wet towel on my side of the bed or use my toothbrush by mistake. If he wasn't so kind, these things would probably drive me crazy.

We've learned that it's easy to be kind when things are going well—and when your partner is being kind first. It's a different story, however, when things aren't going so well—or when your partner isn't being so nice. This, however, is the time when it's most important to practice kindness. In fact, these are some of the most defining moments of your relationship.

People are like mirrors of one another. For the most part, we get back that which we put out. The next time the person you love is having a bad day, try something a little different. Look him in the eye with a smile that says, "It's okay," and "I love you all the time, even when you're low." Chances are, if you do, you'll get a smile in return. We think you'll agree that kindness, practiced on a daily basis, is one the key ingredients to nourishing your partnership for a lifetime.

8.

DON'T USE YOUR PARTNER
AS A PUNCHING BAG!

Let's face it, most of us like to vent, at least once in a while. It just feels good to get certain things off your chest. And while venting is something that neither of us advocates as a therapeutic technique or as a way to relax, we have to admit that, on occasion, we do it too. For whatever reason, when you're frustrated, it sometimes feels good to share that frustration with someone you love. And even if it doesn't feel good, sometimes you just can't seem to help it.

There's an enormous difference, however, between an occasional venting session where you're letting off steam versus making venting an integral part of your regular communication. We've observed that in relationships where one person is a regular "venter," the other person often reports feeling like a punching bag!

One of the problems with venting is that there's an endless supply of material to vent over. In other words, there will always be things to be upset about if your focus is in that direction. Therefore, if you associate "feeling better" with letting off steam while talking to your partner, it's addictive and easy for it to become a habit. Naturally, your assumption would be that more is better.

It's easy to see why a participant on the listening end of a venting session might begin, especially over time, to feel like a punching bag.

Imagine, for a moment, that you're a little tired at the end of the day. You're feeling relatively peaceful and as if life is treating you well. As you pick up a book and prepare to read for a few minutes before dinner, your partner enters the room and begins to complain about his day.

You love your partner and certainly want to be supportive. You put down your book and begin to listen. During the next ten minutes your mood undergoes an enormous shift. You've been told of many horrible things, reminded of the ills of the world and of how unfair and hard life can be. His arguments are so convincing you're starting to believe it yourself. Ouch, he starts again. He goes on to tell you some negative gossip and several examples of greed. At this moment, it seems that your partner, bless his heart, hates his life. He's told you of the twelve people who have wronged him and the four others he's mad at.

In this example, the "venter" was probably just in a really low mood and feeling sorry for himself. In all likelihood, he will see things differently tomorrow. And certainly, if the listener knew this based on her previous knowledge of him, she probably wouldn't worry about it too much. She could simply listen and be as supportive as possible.

On the other hand, it's difficult to always have the perspective needed not to be brought down by the venting of someone else, especially when it's excessive. So, even though some venting is probably inevitable, there is a bit of selfishness involved as well. In other words, when we vent, someone else may be paying the price. So perhaps the best thing to do is simply be aware of how much venting is okay and how much is too much.

Again, we're not saying it's never a good idea to vent, especially in small doses. However, it's a good idea to keep it under control. Doing so will keep your partner from feeling like a punching bag.

9.

ASK THE QUESTION: WHOSE QUIRK IS THIS, ANYWAY?

(KRIS)

Isn't it usually the day-to-day, wash-the-toothpaste-down-the-sink, close-the-toilet-seat kind of stuff about living with someone that can drive us crazy? It's funny, but you can love someone deeply and still become easily bothered by the simple act of sharing space with them. If the same things are bothering you over and over again, before you make it a real issue, it helps to ask yourself the question, "Whose quirk is this, anyway?"

For many years, as part of my morning ritual, I would go to the linen closet and pick out a fresh colorful towel in preparation for my shower. Inevitably, however, Richard would pop into the shower first. When I got around to my shower, I'd reach out and find that my nice clean towel would be gone. Nearly every morning I found myself running through the house, dripping wet, to get my towel. After a while, it made me crazy!

One day, as I was walking to the linen closet to get my towel, I started to feel angry, even before my shower, anticipating in advance that my fresh towel was shortly going to be, once again, used by my husband. For whatever reason, however, I was blessed that morning with a change of heart. I thought about it for a moment and asked myself two obvious questions, "Well, if I can get one towel, why not get two? Whose quirk is this, anyway?"

From a certain perspective, the scenario was really funny. I was right on the edge of an emotional meltdown, while Richard was oblivious to my frustration. All along, he was thinking what a sweet wife he was married to, to always have a towel ready for him.

The nature of quirks can play out in many ways. I heard the story of a couple, for example, where the wife is relatively clean and the husband is obsessively neat and organized. I mean *really* clean. One night David's wife left a piece of lettuce in the sink after doing the dishes. He stood at the kitchen sink and yelled out at the top of his lungs, "Pamela, are you going to get over here and finish cleaning up your mess in the kitchen?"

Now, whose quirk is this, anyway? Obviously his.

Reflecting on this subject can be incredibly freeing if either person is able to see what's really happening. For example, in this instance, if David was able to see that he is the one who is neurotic, the one with the quirk, he would be able to laugh at himself and stop putting such high expectations on his wife. On the other hand, if Pamela was able to understand David's quirk, and see it as his problem, she would be able to brush it off or simply roll her eyes without taking it too personally.

When it comes to minor everyday irritations, keep in mind that we all have our own little quirks. As in my example, consider the possibility that it may not be what your partner is doing (or isn't doing) that bothers you as much as what you are doing (or not doing). Or, as in the case of David, you might simply have too high an expectation about something.

Often, if you just stop for a moment and reflect on the situation, honestly, and with a little humility, you'll see an obvious solution, or you'll see the situation differently. So when you're feeling bugged, try asking yourself the question, "Whose quirk is this, anyway?" At least some of the time the answer will be, "It's mine."

10.

TALK TO HIM HIS WAY

John Gray makes a great point in his *Men Are from Mars, Women Are from Venus* books that men and women are different. In fact, no two people are alike, and we all see the world through our own vision. We all filter information through a unique screen determined by our own personal history and the way we see the world. It's important to understand your partner's reality in order to effectively communicate with him, or for that matter, to have any chance of having an ongoing loving relationship.

We know a couple where the two partners are complete opposites. Joanne is highly intuitive and creative, and the epitome of a right-brain, emotional thinker. She can make instant, brilliant decisions based solely on her intuition and creativity. Ray is a type A, 100 percent left-brain, analytical thinker. Ray makes a perfect devil's advocate. To him, everything needs to make logical sense or it's disregarded. If he disagrees with something, he will immediately begin thinking of all the reasons why it doesn't make any sense.

When they first met, theirs was a case where opposites definitely attracted one another. Ray loved Joanne's spontaneity and her willingness and ability to enjoy the moment. He felt that he needed to be with someone who was less aggressive and more nurturing than he. Therefore, Joanne was just what the doctor ordered. Likewise, when she first fell in love with Ray,

Joanne loved his intellectual and driven nature. She was impressed with his willingness to work weekends, go without sleep, and spend hours analyzing problems, because these were things she had never been able to do. She felt that they would certainly complement each other and live happily ever after!

Over the years, however, their differences began to eat away at their loving connection. Ray became distant and frustrated because once the novelty wore off and real-life issues presented themselves, he simply couldn't understand Joanne's emotional decision-making process. She would make decisions that, from his perspective, weren't "thought out." This frustrated him no end.

Likewise, Joanne became depressed because she never felt equipped to compete with Ray's methodical and aggressive style of communication. Ray had been the captain of his college debate team, and Joanne would often leave their discussions feeling squashed and dejected, as if she was one of his inferior opponents.

Luckily, Joanne had a major insight. She has discovered a way to empower herself while also strengthening their communication. She realized that their marriage was doomed if she couldn't find a way to talk to Ray, his way—in a way he could really understand. So, today, when a situation arises where she is sure that they will be in conflict, or if she wishes to discuss an uncomfortable or difficult subject, Joanne has learned to outline all of her points and back them up in an organized, linear fashion (to the extent that she is able to do so). She knows that this is the only possible way that Ray will be able to hear what she has to say. It's important to know, however, that Joanne didn't come to this conclusion out of a sense of surrender, but rather from wisdom, as a means of taking their relationship to a new level of partnership. We have learned that speaking to your partner in his or her way all but ensures better communication.

The results have been spectacular. While Ray may not always agree with Joanne's point of view, he has become less judgmental and reactive, and a far better listener. He can process the information in a more businesslike manner, the way he is accustomed to thinking. He has even shown a slight willingness to attempt to speak to Joanne in ways that make her comfortable.

In addition, Joanne now feels equipped to handle his questions without appearing overly emotional. She's encouraged that he seems more willing to listen.

We're not taking the position that all men are more linear in their thinking, or that women are always more emotional. Instead, we're all different in the ways that we think. Knowing this can give you the power to change the dynamics of your relationship, forever. Remember, your reality is not *the* reality—it's just yours. Finding a way to understand your partner is a wise thing to do.

11.

AVOID THE WORDS,
"I LOVE YOU, BUT"

There's no question that three of the most beautiful and longed-for words in any language are "I love you." Left alone, they can bring forth feelings of warmth and connection. However, you can virtually destroy the beauty as well as much of the positive impact of these wonderful words by doing nothing other than adding the word "but" to the end of the phrase. Doing so turns a statement of innocence and respect into a manipulative and self-serving lecture.

Kris was the first woman to teach me this important lesson. Years ago, shortly after we fell in love, she looked me in the eye and asked me the question, "Are you aware that you have qualified your love for me twice in the past five minutes?" At the time, I didn't even know what she meant. She went on to explain that while she appreciated the fact that I enjoyed telling her that I loved her, the truth was that my words seemed far less genuine when I attached a condition. Specifically, I had told her, "I love you, BUT I want you to stop keeping me waiting" and "I love you, BUT it bothers me when you assume I'll want to do something when your friends are involved." Later she told me that she was bringing it up because it was becoming a habit, and she hoped I could nip it in the bud.

When she first brought this to my attention, I was a little defensive. I've since learned, however, that there was no reason to be. Kris wasn't making a statement that she was above criticism, or that I wasn't free to bring up issues that were bugging me. To the contrary, she encouraged it (and still does). What she was asking me to do was to separate my "I love you's" from any issues I was having with her. She was correctly pointing out that while both ends of the spectrum (the expression of love and the freedom to discuss issues) are important in an honest, loving relationship, the two are absolutely unrelated.

As I thought about it, it made perfect sense. When you examine the intent of the word "but" after the words "I love you," it becomes clear that the only reason you would connect the two would be to make your gripe or complaint appear more reasonable. Rather than having the courage to simply bring up the issues that were concerning me, I was making certain that, first, I looked like a good guy. In a way it was like saying, "I'm a really nice, patient, and tolerant guy who really loves you. And now that we've established all of this, let me tell you how I want you to change so that you will be even more loving in my eyes."

If that isn't grotesque, what is? It has "hidden agenda" written all over it!

Since that time, I've heard this "add-on" hundreds, maybe even thousands, of times. Often, as was the case with me, it's delivered directly from one person to his partner. In many other instances it's delivered secondhand. For example, just yesterday I was talking to a woman on the phone who told me, "I really love Kurt, BUT I can't stand it when he interrupts me."

This is a very simple idea that pays enormous dividends. The idea, as Kris originally taught me, is to avoid connecting your loving praise with the things that are bothering you. When you feel love for your partner, tell her. Likewise, when something bothers you, share that too. Just don't do it at the same time. If you're at all like me, you'll soon discover that both your compliments and your concerns will be taken far more seriously.

12.

FILL YOUR LIFE WITH
OPPORTUNITIES TO EXPRESS LOVE

Over the years, many people have shared with us their longing to be "in love." And while we certainly understand the need and desire to be in a love relationship, it's important to know that there are many genuine and powerful ways, other than a romantic relationship, to fill your life with love.

We heard a beautiful and touching story about a friend of a friend. Like many people, she was lonely. She felt empty, as though her life couldn't possibly be complete without someone to share it with. Her friends, of course, offered all sorts of well-meaning advice; they tried to set her up; challenged her to get out more; directed her to clubs, classes, and other traditional ways to meet single people. Nothing did the trick.

Then someone suggested that she volunteer her time. For many reasons, the idea struck a chord, so she began volunteering at a nursing home. This simple act of love was the catalyst to changing her life. To make a long story short, she "fell in love with" (metaphorically) a lovely woman in her nineties. The experience of sharing love and giving love opened her heart in ways she had never imagined. She felt appreciated and honored. Her heart opened, and she began to exude love in all aspects of her life. She felt happier, more peaceful and fulfilled than ever before. She had expanded her definition of love.

The feeling of love is contagious. When your heart is open and you're busy sharing your love with others, you draw more love of all kinds in your direction.

It wasn't long before this woman became involved with a man she had known for a long time, as a friend. Although it would be difficult to quantify, there's no question that her entire presence had changed due to the love that was now in her heart.

Romantic love, a loving partnership, marriage—all are wonderful. The truth is, however, that there are countless ways to express love and to receive love. You can do so with pets, volunteerism, nature, a good cause, even hobbies. Anything you enjoy, that nurtures your spirit in a loving way, that allows you to share your love with something or someone else, has the potential to fill your heart with love. One of the most loving times in my life was back in college. I was volunteering as a big brother for the Big Brothers of America organization. The experience changed my life. I was able to spend time with a wonderful little boy who was only six years old at the time. My guess is that it wasn't a coincidence that I met Kris shortly thereafter.

When we are filled with loving feelings, whether those feelings are directed toward humans, animals, God, nature, or simply a love of life, we put ourselves in a position to attract love. When our heart is filled with love, and we are sharing that love, we become kinder, gentler, and more patient. Our perspective is enhanced and we become more satisfied.

Often, when we're only looking to be loved, it's easy to forget how wonderful it is to give love. Yet, when we discover new ways to share our love, an almost magical transformation takes place in our lives. We become more interested in others, more inclusive and wiser. It almost seems like a law of nature—the more ways we discover to express, share, and be loving, the more we find ourselves surrounded by the feeling of love.

Whether you're in a romantic relationship or not, or whether you want to be in one or not, isn't critical. Whatever your circumstances, dreams, or preferences, filling your life with opportunities to express your love is always a good idea.

13.

LOOK FOR THE GIFTS

The human mind is an amazing thing in that, whatever it's looking for, it tends to find. So, if you're looking for ugliness, you'll have no trouble finding it. If you're looking for cruelty, again, you'll find plenty of evidence of that, too. And if you're looking for beauty, you'll be able to find that, as well.

Without question, one of the most effective ways to immunize yourself from the usual frustrations of being in a relationship, as well as one of the best ways to keep your relationship lighthearted and vibrant, is to use this predictable mental dynamic as a tool to look for and identify the gifts that often are cleverly disguised as hassles or emergencies. This is a practical way to keep your heart open and to grow from, rather than be frustrated by, day-to-day living.

There are endless examples of how to use this strategy to enhance your relationship, even in scenarios that ordinarily would seem painful or cause for alarm. Here are just a few:

Suppose your partner is flirting with a good-looking stranger. What possible gift could be found in something like this? You could, of course, use this as an excuse to fly into a jealous rage or to confront your mate. Either way, your relationship will probably suffer some degree of damage. Looked at as a gift, however, it might be seen as a "wake-up call," a sign that you need to be more attentive and loving, a gift that might transform or even save your relationship.

Imagine that your wife is offered a job in a different part of the country. This could be seen as a major hassle or even a tragedy. If you focus on this aspect of it and express this position, you'll probably feel bad or be seen as an unsupportive spouse. If you were looking for a gift, however, it might be seen as an ideal chance to demonstrate how supportive you can be, or as an opportunity to begin a new adventure together.

A couple who had been married for twenty years approached me after a lecture. With his wife standing by his side, smiling, the husband told me that he had suffered an injury that probably would make him impotent for life. He went on to say that it had turned out to be one of the most important things that had ever happened to him. Prior to the injury, he had become single-minded in his career ambition to the point of becoming almost uncommunicative. The two of them were drifting apart, and the only intimacy they experienced together was, occasionally, in the bedroom—hardly nourishing enough to hold together a twenty-year-old marriage. The injury had forced him (and them) to learn new ways to feel and express intimacy. After twenty years, the two of them had finally learned to become friends. His wife said that he has turned out to be "one of the kindest men in the world." Certainly, it was a sacrifice and had required adjustments, but according to her, "The accident turned out to be a gift in disguise."

It seems that if there are people wise and resilient enough to see a gift in something seemingly so painful, then the rest of us ought to be able to discover the gifts in most of our more ordinary day-to-day experiences. The truth is, we can when it's our intention to do so.

When you're looking for the gifts in a situation, you'll almost always be able to find something positive to focus on. When this becomes your normal way of perceiving things, you'll find that it's almost impossible to get too upset over daily things, especially "small stuff."

14.

MARK YOUR CALENDAR

(KRIS)

Let's face it: Premenstrual syndrome, or PMS, is real. I know, because every month since I was a young teen (other than when I was pregnant), I've had it. And chances are, if you're a woman, you have had it too. It's one of those unavoidable aspects of being female.

Over the years, I've learned that when my thoughts start getting a little crazy or when I'm in a particularly melancholy mood, I take a look at my calendar, and lo and behold, it's usually a week or so before my period. Everyday, ordinary events that are usually taken in stride suddenly seem like irritants or emergencies.

As if it wasn't bad enough to go through PMS yourself, it's even worse that your partner has to share this experience with you. Virtually every month for the first ten years of our relationship, Richard would ask me lovingly, "Kris, what's wrong?" Finally, one day, in the midst of my PMS, I screamed, "Please take a look at your calendar! There is nothing wrong!"

It's important for women not to use PMS as an ongoing excuse to blow up, or for irrational behavior. On the other hand, it's helpful to become aware of your symptoms and to understand that what you are feeling, due to PMS, makes everything look worse than it really is; little things are blown out of proportion and it's easy to sweat the small stuff!

Understanding this helps you make certain allowances for the way you are feeling. You can begin to understand that, despite the urgency and frustration you feel, things are not as bad as they seem. PMS might be seen as the ultimate form of a low mood. And, as in any low mood, the best you can usually do is understand that "this too shall pass."

Sharing this information with your partner will help him understand these timely and predictible moods you go through. You'll find it enormously helpful if both of you make a mental note or mark your calendar. Ideally, each of you can make special allowances during this difficult time and, hard as it may be, try to be extra compassionate and patient.

Marking my calendar helps to soften my fuse and helps Richard understand and remain compassionate when I say something a little off the wall or when my temper is shorter than usual. I see the PMS part of my cycle as a low cloud (sometimes a thunderstorm) that passes by. I've learned that it's important to keep your perspective about life during these times. With perspective and awareness, you realize that, despite what it looks and feels like, life really hasn't temporarily gone crazy. This reminds you that your ability to deal with stress will soon return to normal.

15.

SHARE AN INSIGHT

An extremely effective way to learn to stop sweating the small stuff is to share an experience with one another. You can share with your partner a time when you responded with grace rather than hostility to something that would normally bug you. Or, you might share an insight you experienced regarding a certain way to make your life less stressful, or a new way to look at a problem or a frustration.

The reason this process is so powerful is that it helps you put more emphasis and attention on what's right with your relationship and with your life—what's working, what you're grateful about, and what's not bothering you—these and other factors that keep you from sweating the small stuff. It also brings to the surface ideas and tips on how each of you can become more relaxed and loving.

Jennifer had spent most of her life "holding on" to things that bothered her. Usually, when someone would do something she didn't like, she would hold a grudge, or at least hold it against that person for a long, long time. At times, this made her come across as harsh and demanding.

One day, however, all of that began to change. Someone at work had taken credit for an idea that she had developed. To make matters worse, her co-worker not only stole her idea, but was offered a special project in recognition of her "creative thinking."

Even if she wanted to, there was nothing Jennifer could do about it, as there was no realistic way to prove the injustice. For a while she fell into her old habit and was furious. She was playing out a war (with her co-worker) in her mind, thinking of ways she might retaliate.

Then, she had an insight. She realized that her own thinking was making matters worse than they already were and that she was blowing the incident out of proportion. She decided that she was tired of being angry and resentful and that she was finally ready to try something different. For a long time, Jennifer wanted to be happy. She had been reading about the power of forgiveness and had understood it, on an intellectual level. However, until this experience, she hadn't been able to put forgiveness into practice. Because of the blatant nature of the situation, she decided that this was the perfect opportunity to practice it.

She decided to forgive, and as soon as she did, her heart began to open. She began to relax, just enough to become more accepting of the situation and to let go of her resentment. She realized that a vast majority of the time people were honest and didn't steal ideas from her, or others. Further, she came to the conclusion that the person who stole her idea needed not hatred, but compassion.

Jennifer shared her insight of forgiveness with her boyfriend, Steve. He was so impressed with her ability to open her heart in a difficult situation that it opened the door to a brand-new type of communication between them. Steve had been a student of spirituality for quite some time and was a relatively easygoing person. His only hesitancy in committing his life to Jennifer was that he was concerned that she had a tendency to hold grudges. He had often wondered if she would ever be able to break this habit.

The new level of depth in their communication and in their relationship was impressive. It led to other instances when Jennifer was able to choose forgiveness over resentment. Her growth was so dramatic that it spawned insights for Steve, as well. The success built on itself and deepened their relationship.

This story has a happy ending. It wasn't too long before the two became engaged and eventually married. Although there obviously are many factors that create a permanent bond, both Jennifer and Steve traced the ultimate success of their relationship back to that single incident, the sharing of an insight.

The nice things about insights is that they tend to feed upon themselves, particularly when shared with a loved one. It makes you wonder what good things might be in store for the rest of us if we choose to share our insights with our partner.

16.

STAY AWAY FROM ULTIMATUMS

I once did a survey, asking one hundred people if they liked it when they were given an ultimatum. Ninety-five people said no. The other five said some variation of "You must be kidding." The next time I did the survey, I rephrased the question. This time I asked, "Can you think of an instance where you would appreciate being given an ultimatum if there were any other options?" Slightly different question—exact same answer. I've never met anyone who likes ultimatums. Have you? Yet, many people use this form of manipulation on a regular basis to get what they want. My experience is that, in one way or another, it almost always backfires.

This isn't to say there aren't certain instances when you have virtually no option but to give someone an ultimatum—for example, "You must show up to work on time or you're going to lose your job." That's a different issue. What we are talking about here is the fact that, in relationships, ultimatums rarely are well received.

There are several good reasons to stay away from ultimatums. First, ultimatums box people into a corner and limit and distort their choices. An aggressive and obnoxious sense of pressure is added to an already difficult decision, which seems to create an almost universal repulsion.

Second, even if the person demanding the ultimatum ends up getting what he or she wants, they are often resented and retaliated against by the person to whom they issued the ultimatum. For example, Jean says to Robert, "If you don't agree to attend my family reunion I won't talk to you for a week and you can forget about borrowing my car." Robert may end up going—but resent the entire trip and harbor negative thoughts about Jean for a long time to come. He may find ways to "get back at her" and may even lose respect for her for painting him into a corner.

In the long run, a more effective way to ask would have been for Jean to say, "I'd really love for you to be there with me. I hate to put such pressure on you, but I have to admit that I'll be very disappointed if you don't come."

Not always, but often, an ultimatum stems from the fear that, in the absence of the ultimatum, you're not going to get what you want. So, out of desperation, you demand it, attaching a serious consequence—hoping that will do the trick. The problem is, you push the person away far more often than you frighten someone into doing it your way.

A man I used to know whose name was Roger was crazy about his girl-friend, Ann. He really wanted to get married and Ann was leaning in that direction, but wasn't quite ready. He gave her the very common ultimatum, "Marry me now or it's over." You know the rest of the story. Years later, Roger was still upset that Ann didn't marry him, while she was happily married to someone else with two beautiful children. The sad part of this story is that, had Roger simply been more patient and loving, Ann probably would have been ready for marriage within a reasonable amount of time. Even if she had decided not to marry Roger, he still would have been better off, as she would have ended the relationship with more respect and fonder memories for him. As it turned out, she couldn't stand the pressure and left with a feeling of disgust.

As I mentioned above, there are certain instances where a person has no option other than to give an ultimatum. For example, what if you really want to get married and have a family—and your partner, even after years together, simply won't make the commitment? In this type of situation it's probably necessary. But if you have to do it, at least explain to your partner that you wish you didn't have to. Acknowledge that you understand the distasteful nature of ultimatums.

What's most important here is to simply see that it's best to avoid ultimatums whenever possible. You'll probably end up getting more of what you want anyway—and without question, your relationship will be on a more solid footing. So stop giving ultimatums—or else!

17.

ALLOW TIME FOR
TRANSITIONS

There are many periods of transition in a long-term relationship. These are often brought on by the "big stuff" that happens to you: things like the commitment of a new marriage, pregnancy and the introduction of a child to your life, moving, changing jobs, the death of a loved one, retirement, or an empty nest. These and other major changes present challenges to your relationships. We've found that the most graceful way to move through these transitions is to make allowances for them by allowing plenty of time. When you make the assumption that a transition is going to take time, it seems to take the urgency, as well as much of the frustration, out of the picture. It allows you the time to adjust and settle in.

The addition of a child to your family is, for example, one of the biggest changes any couple will have to adapt to. Many relationships are not prepared for the emotional introduction of a child and what that means to their life as a couple. Parents often differentiate between B.K. (before kids) and A.K. (after kids). One thing is certain here: You won't truly understand what they are talking about until you go through it. The same is true, of course, with all major transitions. It's impossible for someone to understand the difficulty of being relocated to a new city where you don't know anyone, unless you've been through it.

Bringing home a newborn baby is, without a doubt, one of the most magical periods in your life. It isn't, however, without many new challenges. The stress of sleep deprivation and adjusting to the physical demands of caring for this little person can test even the most settled couples. In addition, it's an awkward time for some men. While some may thrive on watching their wives nurture another soul, others will feel isolated and left out during this first year.

Looking back, it's clear to us that one of the reasons we made it through this period of time so well was that we made a commitment, together, that we would allow plenty of time for the transition. We agreed that we wouldn't expect our lives to be the same, and we decided to avoid comparing our life to the way it used to be. This decision proved to be very comforting and helpful. As new events would unfold, we were able, for the most part, to accept and embrace them for what they were, instead of becoming frustrated by our lack of familiarity.

We've shared this philosophy with many young couples who are bringing a new baby into their lives. Almost without exception, we've been told that it was very helpful.

We've found that the same idea applies to virtually all periods of transition. Two of our dearest friends were transferred to a new location. They had a young child and were concerned about the move. They were unfamiliar with the new city and initially had no friends. Rather than become despondent or frightened, however, they decided to embrace the philosophy of allowing time for their transition. To their delight, it worked wonders. Rather than expecting their lives to instantly be as fulfilling as before, they created an artificial time frame of transition. They decided they wouldn't expect to feel settled for at least a year. Then, with each new friend they met and each positive experience they had, they were delighted and grateful. They eased into their new lives and are now happier than ever before.

Transitions are like speed bumps: You need to slow down while approaching them. Rather than expecting your life to remain the same, or trying to recreate the life you are most familar with, try to be open and accepting to change. If, instead of panicking, you allow for plenty of time for your transitions, you will, like a dancer, gracefully adjust to the next step in the process.

18.

DON'T FIGHT UNLESS
THE MOOD IS RIGHT

Moods are really funny things. On one hand, when your mood is up and you're feeling good, life looks pretty darn good. Generally speaking, your relationship looks pretty good too. You feel secure, loving, and satisfied. You tend to think about the nice aspects of your relationship—you feel secure and you keep your sense of humor. You understand that while no relationship is perfect or trouble-free, you are lucky to be with the one you love. You see his or her strengths as charming and delightful, and the inevitable flaws as relatively insignificant. You see even the quirks as more evidence that your partner, like you, is a unique character, and overall, you're lucky to have one another. You find it easy to compromise and forgive, and you let go of the little day-to-day stuff quickly without excessive thought. You don't feel defensive and, in fact, can usually see where you are contributing to any problems you might be having. You remember the good times and look forward to a bright future.

On the other hand, when your mood is down and you're feeling grumpy, agitated, and stressed, your life looks drastically different—particularly your relationships. All of a sudden, you're feeling dissatisfied, as if something is missing. Little annoyances seem like they must be the tip of the iceberg of something far more significant. Rather than letting things go, you start to analyze your issues. You mostly think about the aspects of your relationship that aren't quite right, and you lose your sense of gratitude. In fact, you become quite picky and start to take your partner for granted. You lose your ability to see your contribution to any communication or other problems you might be having—everything seems like it's his fault. Your partner's strengths seem to disappear, and the flaws jump out at you in dramatic fashion. Rather than being able to compromise, you become stubborn and defensive. You remember the bad times, and your future looks bleak!

When you step back and think about it, moods are bizarre. After all, it's the exact same life—and the exact same partner! The same person—with the same history, personality, strengths, and weaknesses. The person looks the same, has the same quirks, habits, and voice. Yet, despite everything being essentially identical from one moment to the next, your mood—like an optical illusion—has the power to alter your perspective to the point of convincing you that things are different from what they really are. But whereas an optical illusion merely tricks your vision, your mood tricks your judgment, perspective, feelings of love, even your memory.

But there's hope! Despite their apparent power, the effect of moods on your relationship can be minimized. All that is required is a respect for the illusion of moods along with the willingness to make certain allowances for your moods—and your partner's moods—when they occur. In other words, your moods are going to continue to come and go as they always have, but you can learn to respond to them in an entirely new way. Rather than reacting with a familiar knee-jerk reaction—that is, becoming defensive, hostile, jealous, picky, or in some other way reactive—you can instead say to yourself, "I know I'm in a low mood and I'm not seeing things as they really are at this moment." You take a step back and make allowances for the fact that you're in a negative state of mind. You distrust your reactions. Rather than thinking, "This relationship is going nowhere," you instead say to yourself, "Of course I'm assuming the worst—as I often do—when I'm feeling this way." Or instead of thinking, "My partner is the worst listener in the world," you remember that you never feel listened to in a negative state of mind.

Your awareness of the deceptive nature of low moods can eliminate a great deal of frustration—and will most certainly keep you from blowing many things out of proportion. Reactivity will be replaced by compassion. When your partner snaps at you, for example, rather than taking it personally and thinking something like, "He always does that," you'll remember that everyone snaps or acts less than loving once in a while, especially when they are feeling badly.

An understanding of moods is not a prescription for accepting bad behavior or for pretending things are better than they really are. Instead, it's a helpful tool that keeps you from sweating the small stuff and for keeping your perspective. Everyone, including you, will say and do things in a low mood that would never even occur to them in a higher mood. Keep in mind that if you are in a bad mood and you're upset about something, that something—whatever it is—will still be there when your mood rises. Therefore, if you let it go and make the decision to take it less seriously—at least for now—you will become far more immune to the negative effects of your (or your partner's) moods. The key is to wait, to understand that your perspective is being influenced by your mood. Instead of analyzing your life in these moments, be grateful. Soon, you'll be feeling better again.

When you're feeling good again, more secure and loving—when your mood is right—feel free to discuss your issues, share your dissatisfactions, and think about your problems. You'll find that in most cases, whatever was bothering you has probably disappeared or at least seems far less significant. And in those cases where you're still feeling bothered, you'll have far more wisdom and common sense available to you. So, go ahead and fight—but wait until the mood is right.

19.

KNOW YOUR OWN VALUE

Ideally, everyone who is in a love relationship would treat their partner as a 100 percent equal, in every sense of the word. Unfortunately, however, we don't live in an ideal world. For a variety of reasons, there are some people, both men and women, who feel a sense of superiority. In some cases, they feel their role or contribution is more significant or important than their partner's. In other cases there is simple ignorance. Then there are those who have an unhealthy dose of arrogance or self-importance.

One of the greatest gifts you can give yourself and, ultimately, your relationship is to know your own value, to feel secure that you are special, unique, and important. There isn't a person in this world who is just like you, and no one could take your place. Your contribution is important, and the gifts and value you bring to your relationship are significant and irreplaceable.

Sadly, there are many people who buy into their partner's sense of self-importance. Perhaps their partner makes most or all of the family income, so they feel (and are often treated) as dependant. The wage earner acts as if their partner is lucky to be "taken care of" and minimizes their contribution. And while a person is fortunate to have their material needs met by his or her partner, it's equally true that the "breadwinner" is every bit as fortunate to have many of his or her needs met as well. Often, it's the non-breadwinner, behind the scenes, who makes it possible and convenient for the breadwinner to do his or her thing. To minimize this part of the puzzle is selfish and foolish.

An incredible shift takes place when both partners know their own value, when each person feels secure in their unique contribution. It's nourishing to a relationship when each person feels he or she is an equal partner.

I met a couple who fits one of the classic "stereotypical" models. Sean, the husband, worked outside of the home and earned the family income. Martha stayed home with their three school-age children. Both worked extremely hard. The primary difference between the two was that, while Martha appreciated her husband's contribution, Sean took Martha for granted, in every sense of the word. He did little, if anything, around the house. When one of the kids would get sick in the middle of the night, he assumed she would take care of it while he slept soundly. Any and all hassles were hers to deal with. His attitude spoke as loudly as his actions. She claimed it was somewhat subtle, yet in a way, he spoke down to Martha, almost as if to "keep her in her place."

The difference between this couple and so many others, and the reason we wanted to include their story in this book, is that Martha never, for a moment, doubted her own value. For years she put up with her husband's arrogance, thinking he (to use her words) "just didn't get it." At some point, however, she became fed up.

Rather than feel badly about herself or their marriage, Martha took matters into her own hands. She didn't sulk, scream, or feel insecure in any way. Instead, she confidently laid down the law. Specifically, she said, "Listen, Sean, I have loved and supported you for a long, long time. I know you have some strange guy thing where you feel your contribution is more important than mine, but you're just plain wrong! In fact, you're out-to-lunch. I don't know of a gentle way to put this, so I'm just going to come out and say it. I'm taking a one-month vacation from doing things for you. If you get the message, I'll go back to my old ways; if not, you're on your own for another month. During this month you'll have no meals cooked for you, no laundry, no reminders of your commitments and absolutely no cleaning of any kind. If the house is a mess, you can clean it up or not—I don't care. I won't cover for you when you miss important activities the kids are involved with, nor will I track down the numerous things you seem to lose every day. I'll continue doing the fifty or so things I always do for the kids because I love them and they are too young to fully appreciate all I do for them, but you have no excuse. I want you to know that I still love you very much, but I'm not playing anymore. Good luck and have a nice month."

Unbelievably, Martha stuck to her guns for the entire month! When she told me the story, I wondered how their marriage survived—but it did. After his initial resentment and shock, Sean developed a new respect for his wife which, apparently, changed the dynamics of their marriage. In fact, he looks back shamefully at his old attitude.

Obviously, this is an extreme case, and Martha's approach wouldn't work for, or even appeal to, everyone. In fact, I've never heard another story quite like it. However, it demonstrates the power of knowing your own value. Hopefully, your partner (man or woman) would never minimize your value for any reason, financial or otherwise. However, even if this happens, it's helpful to remember that how you feel about yourself is what's most important. Take time on a regular basis to remind yourself how special and wonderful you really are. If you do, you'll always know your own value.

20.

PUT A POSITIVE SPIN ON IT

In politics, the term *spin* has taken on a negative connotation. Whether conservative or liberal, the term implies a false or misleading "slant" with self-interest in mind. In personal relationships, however, it's a far different story. The idea of putting a positive spin on the events, circumstances, and challenges of your relationship can become one of the most important habits you can incorporate into your life together. In fact, in the absence of this habit, virtually anything—big or small—has the power to upset or frustrate you.

So much of our experience depends on how we look at it. There's a story of two male bricklayers who have identical jobs. Someone asks the first man, "What is it that you do?" He answers in a negative tone, obviously feeling sorry for himself: "I sit here every day laying one stupid brick on top of another." The man turns to the other bricklayer and asks the same question. His response is quite different. He says in a confident, upbeat manner, "I am a craftsman. I help build all the beautiful buildings you see around you. Without my contribution, none of this would be here."

The moral of the story is that both men are right!

We met a couple who had lost everything they owned in a horrible fire. They decided it was a blessing in disguise. Their position was that it gave them a chance to start over and to rebuild their lives together from the ground up, literally!

We met another couple who lost their life savings to a slimy con scheme. Yet, rather than let it ruin their lives and make them feel like bitter victims, they made a different decision. They decided that they had become too greedy and materialistic. This event, painful as it was, was their chance to reevaluate their priorities and live a much simpler life.

The same facts could, and often do, tear couples apart.

Yet, it's easy to see that you can take almost any situation and look at it in two ways. You can look for what's in it for you, any hidden gifts that might be found, and for what you can learn from it. Or you can take the more common view and see virtually all difficulties and hassles as simply more evidence that life is hard and unfair.

Obviously, reading this strategy doesn't mean you'll always be able to look at events from a more positive perspective (we can't either), but it's sure comforting to know that the possibility exists.

Whether it's something relatively minor—your date shows up late or stands you up, your husband has too much to drink one night, your wife flirts with another man, your spouse isn't pulling his weight with the household chores—or something more serious—your child gets into a little trouble, you are forced to relocate to a new city, one of you loses your job, or you suffer a physical problem—you always have the option of putting a positive slant on it, once you think you do.

You could say, "Oh sure, that's pie-in-the-sky thinking." But you might want to ask yourself, "What options do I have?" The only option we're aware of is to be negative—to put a defeatist, pessimistic slant on it. But when you think about it, that's not a very good option. All this does is make any situation worse and harder to deal with than it already is. It also tends to make everyone around you feel depressed and insecure, and decreases your chances of getting through the situation gracefully or effectively.

Our experience has been that whenever we are able to put a positive slant on a situation—whatever it is—it helps us to grow as a couple, come up with creative solutions, and keep things in perspective. It keeps bad days from becoming worse and difficult experiences from tearing us down. Mostly, it keeps us from sweating the small stuff. So, our position is clear—whenever possible, it's always best to put a positive slant on your experiences.

21.

REMEMBER THAT YOUR PARTNER
CAN'T READ YOUR MIND

It seems to us that one of the worst mistakes many of us make in our relationships is that, without even knowing it, we assume, at times, that our partner can read our mind. Or, if we don't assume they can do so, we very often expect them to.

I was talking to a friend when he started to complain of his wife's inability to stay organized. He seemed tormented by the issue and, in fact, he had brought this subject to my attention on several previous occasions. Finally, I asked him, "Does Carol know how much this bugs you?" It turned out that she had no idea that it concerned him in the least!

There are several good reasons why it's important to recognize this problem, and to nip it in the bud. First, and most obviously, it creates a great deal of grief and inner turmoil for yourself. You carry around a ton of frustration that has little, if anything, to do with you. You're mad, bothered, or irritated about something—and you're the only one who knows about it. If that isn't self-induced stress, what is?

Second, it's not really fair to your partner. Here you are steaming mad about something, and you don't even give your partner the courtesy of telling her what it is that's bugging you. You're probably coming across as mad or irritated, but she doesn't even know what it's about. In cases like these, you're demanding that she read your mind! What chance does she have? How can she explain herself, much less do anything about it?

The first thing that bothered me about Kris was her tendency to keep me waiting. After a while I started fuming about it. I told my good friends; I sulked, complained, and wished she would change. Finally, when I couldn't stand it any longer, I brought it up to her. In a very sincere, nondefensive tone, she said, "I'm really sorry. I didn't even realize I was doing it. I wish you would have told me sooner." It turned out that while I was obsessively punctual, she was quite comfortable running a few minutes behind schedule. She simply didn't think that it was a big deal and had no idea it was bothering me. So, while keeping people waiting may not be a great idea, clearly the responsibility of dealing with the issue was in my hands. I was expecting Kris to read my mind. And while she has many magical qualities, reading my mind is not one of them.

What we've learned is that, when something is bothering you, it's usually best to let your partner know about it. Pick a time when neither of you is in a defensive mood. Then bring up the issue gently and respectfully and see what happens. It seems logical that, in most cases, your chances of a favorable outcome are far better than if you rely on your partner reading your mind. If at all possible, avoid the self-destructive thought, "He (or she) should know what I want or need." You'll make it easier on yourself and on your relationship if you go ahead and let them know.

22.

SET A GOOD EXAMPLE
(KRIS)

We've all heard it said that you can't change other people. It's a strange thing, though. After being in a relationship for some time, we all seem to find things that we'd like to change, don't we? However, as understandable and seductive as it can be to try to change your partner, the fact remains that setting a good example yourself is the best way to influence change in your partner.

We have a friend who loves to read inspirational and spiritual books. She was already a happy and extremely loving person. Her husband, on the other hand, who could really benefit from some sage advice, resisted her requests to read with her—until he was ready. At first, she made the common mistake of insisting that he read her books. And, of course, the more she insisted, the more he resisted and pushed her (and the books) away. It seems to be human nature that nobody likes to have things crammed down their throat.

After awhile, she backed off and continued her own personal studies, letting go of the idea that she would change him. Instead, she continued working on herself. She became calmer and even kinder and happier than she already was. After a while, her happy spirit became a little contagious and her husband became curious. Her good example prompted him to become interested in her books. Today, they have conversations inspired by Dr. Laura, John Gray, and many others.

Another set of friends provide an excellent example of the importance of setting a good example. Barbara has spent a great part of her life studying and practicing health and fitness. She is a beautiful physical specimen. Don, her husband, had focused most of his energy, in recent years, on his career. There came a time a few years ago that it became necessary, for health reasons, for Don to adopt a new, drastically different lifestyle.

Barbara, who was the epitome of health, realized that the only way Don would adhere to the strict vegetarian diet ordered by his doctor was if she adopted it too, which is exactly what she did. Rather than badger him about it, she decided to set the good example. And boy, did it work. Today, both Barbara and Don are visions of excellent health. They are happy, healthy, and vibrant.

I have noticed, over the years, that Richard often follows my lead on certain things. If I eat healthy food and work out a lot, Richard does too. Likewise, the opposite is also true. When I was pregnant, Richard gained a few pounds.

This strategy also pertains to happiness. Over the years, I have watched Richard gracefully move through his high and low moods; he has taught me, by example, to do the same. Rather than lecture me, he simply shows me.

Mental health, loving energy, and good habits are contagious. If there's something in your partner you'd like to see change, take stock of yourself first. Set the example by the way you live, and eventually your partner may come around too.

23.

DON'T FIGHT OVER
STUPID THINGS

This strategy speaks right to the heart of the matter. Fighting over stupid things is another way of saying you're sweating the small stuff—big time! Yet, we see it all the time: couples arguing and bickering over the most ridiculous things. People argue over who misplaced the scissors, whose turn it is to take out the trash, which one of you has more free time, who works harder, or whether or not you had fun at last year's family reunion! People argue over who is a better driver or a more dedicated parent, or who came in second place in a contest that took place last year. People get furious over having to wait a few minutes when their partner is running a little late, when their table manners fall short of perfection, or when their partner misinterprets a fact. We even know a woman who started a fight because her husband put the towels in the wrong bathroom! Wow. What could possibly be more significant than that?

Ironically, many couples will tell you that they rarely bicker over truly significant issues. So it seems to make sense that if one or both persons in a relationship could eliminate all fights (give or take a few) over stupid things, all would be well—at least most of the time.

When you eliminate (or even greatly reduce) the number of little things that bother you enough to fight about, it opens the door to a different kind of relationship. It's so much fun to be around someone who isn't always bothered by something—it's refreshing, inviting, and nourishing. When you refuse to fight over stupid things, you can become true pals again—partners in every sense of the word.

When things don't get to you so much, when your patience and perspective are intact, you reinforce (or remind) your partner why he or she is so fond of you—your sense of humor begins to come out, you become more interesting and introspective, and you're just plain more fun to be around.

Both of us have always made the assumption that a good relationship is something people crave for many reasons—not the least of which is that when you're with someone who isn't easily bothered, who doesn't sweat the small stuff in love, it's extremely stress-reducing because you know it's okay to be yourself in your partner's presence—it's okay to be human. But this gift goes both ways. In other words, you not only want to be around someone who makes life seem easier and more fun, but you also want to be one of those people for your partner. If you can become less inclined to fight over silly little things, you will become far more desirable to your partner in every sense of the word.

Remember that, far from being stress-reducing, it's stress-producing and a real drag to be around someone who is always irritated at something you're doing and always picking a fight over some stupid thing. Why would you even want to be around someone who is always a second away from starting a fight? It's no fun, and it's incredibly stressful.

The solution is really quite simple; mostly it involves intention. The trick, it seems, is to begin to see irrelevant and unimportant things in their proper perspective. It's helpful to reflect on those things that are really important and to make a commitment to let go of almost everything else. Ask yourself the question, "Do I want my life to be about fighting over stupid things and demanding that everyone else, especially the people I love, be

65

different?" By simply asking this question in such a direct and honest manner, the answer will become an obvious . . . no.

You'll begin to see that when you get annoyed and bothered enough to fight over stupid things, what you're really doing is defining yourself as a partner who is unable to stay focused on the gifts and strengths of your relationship. This can be a humbling, if not frightening, realization. Yet, it's an important insight. Because once you turn your judgments around in this manner and see how you are contributing to the problem, you can begin to shift away from this tendency—and instead learn to let the little things go and remain focused on what's right in your relationship. It's that simple.

We can't tell you how much more love you will experience and how much more fun you will have when you put this strategy into practice. From now on, when you catch yourself fighting over stupid little things, laugh at yourself and let it go. Make being happy more important than being stubborn. Soon this could be a habit that will change the course of your relationship forever.

24.

BECOME A
WORLD-CLASS LISTENER

One of the most consistent "sore spots" of relationships is the complaint, "He (or she) doesn't really listen to me." When you ask around, it becomes clear that almost no one feels that their partner is an "expert" listener.

Becoming a world-class listener does two things. First, and most obviously, it nourishes your partner by demonstrating on a moment-to-moment basis that you truly care about what she has to say. It's the best and perhaps only effective way to show that you are interested and that you understand. You can always say, "I care about you," but if your attention is elsewhere, you are demonstrating that other things—those worthy of your attention—are actually more important.

Being a good listener also reinforces the fact that you care about your partner's feelings and that you acknowledge and value her opinions. When someone feels listened to, it contributes to making them feel special instead of taken for granted. Good listening skills encourage the person who is talking to open up and be willing to share, and almost always brings two people closer together. It also encourages reciprocal listening, which creates heartfelt and intimate communication. There's no doubt about it, it's relaxing and engaging to be around someone who listens to you and, quite frankly, it's a drag to be around someone who doesn't.

There is another, perhaps lesser-known, benefit to excellent listening skills to be aware of as well. Effective listening greatly reduces your propensity to overreact to, or get upset by, little things. When you listen carefully and lovingly to your partner, it will, in most cases, prevent you from jumping to conclusions or reacting habitually, which is precisely what happens when you assume you already know what your partner is going to say, or when your mind is drifting, however slightly.

When you take the time and effort to listen, you'll hear (and sense) things you wouldn't otherwise hear if you were simply waiting for your turn to talk, or only partially paying attention to what is being said. You'll become far more compassionate because you'll hear the pain and frustration that is sometimes experienced by your partner. You'll see the innocence in your partner, and your heart will remain open. On the flip side, you'll also be able to share in your partner's joy because you'll hear enthusiasm and excitement that is entirely absent without excellent listening.

The difference between adequate listening and world-class listening is enormous. Often, it can be the difference between a relationship that is poor or that simply seems "okay"—and one that is truly magnificent. Adequate (or normal) listening is often tolerated, but it does nothing to nourish the spirit. Being listened to is such a profound human need that, in its absence, there is almost always a feeling that something is missing. On the other hand, when someone feels heard, as long as it's genuine, she tends to feel complete and satisfied, as if there's nowhere else she'd rather be than right there with you.

The only way to become an expert listener is the old-fashioned way—lots of practice. World-class listening means much more than being able to repeat what your partner has just said. It involves being truly "present" with what is being discussed, as well as being patient and empathetic. It means you first attempt to understand what is being said—you nonjudgmentally internalize it and make sure your partner finished—before you jump in and take your turn.

The good news is, anyone can become a better listener, simply by having the genuine desire to do so. All you have to do is observe how tempting it is to butt in, interrupt, or offer some feedback before the person with whom you're speaking is finished and before you understand what he is trying to say. You'll probably have to catch yourself many times before your habit is under control, but it will get easier with each passing day. As you nip this problem in the bud and as you become at least as interested in listening as you are in speaking, you'll be paving the way to a rare treat—a mutually respectful and satisfying relationship grounded in world-class listening. What could be better than that?

25.

EXPERIENCE A SUDDEN SHIFT

♥ In an earlier book, I mentioned that Jim and Yvonne were married for thirty-two mostly unhappy years when they discovered that Jim had a cancerous, life-threatening tumor. Prior to receiving the bad news, their relationship had been tense and less than loving. They were constantly bickering and irritable at one another. There was plenty of conflict, anger, and frustration, but very little laughter or mutual love and respect. They were often on each other's nerves, and both were constantly sweating the small stuff. Although they were "going through the motions," Jim described their love as having been "lost" for many years. Yvonne agreed.

A strange thing happened, however, when their doctor delivered the news. Their love for one another, which had been swallowed up with bitterness and negativity, suddenly returned—along with their perspective and gratitude. They experienced what might be called a change of heart or a sudden shift. Most of the things that seemed to be keeping them apart and that seemed so irritating and pressing—suddenly seemed insignificant. Like a dark cloud parting to allow the sun to shine, it was as though years of ill feelings disappeared, replaced with warmth and love.

Jim and Yvonne were the same two people with the same habits and the same history as they were before they got the news. They had the same quirks and physical appearances. Certainly their circumstances didn't improve! If anything, they got worse. After all, they were just informed of a terminal illness. Yet, they were filled with a genuine and deep love for each other. Why?

The only thing that changed was their awareness of an illness. In other words, the shift that occurred was entirely mental; they realized they had been acting ridiculously. And because all sudden shifts are mental, it's clear that it doesn't necessarily have to take bad news to experience one. Rather, all it takes is the genuine desire, openness, and willingness to see things differently, as well as a little humility, the willingness to admit that you must be stuck seeing something in a way that is hurting rather than helping your relationship or some other aspect of your life.

It's helpful to state what you'd ideally like to see happen. For example, you might say, "I know it must be me, but I don't know what's going on. I'd sure like to stop feeling and acting so defensive around my partner when she makes a suggestion." An insight may occur—minutes, days, weeks, even months later. But when it hits you, it really hits you. For instance, you might suddenly realize that your partner has a habit of making certain types of comments to everyone she meets and that they aren't intended to be personal to anyone, including you. This insight might give you a sudden sense of perspective, which frees you from feeling defensive around her—an insight that could change the course of your entire relationship. A sudden shift can occur anytime, anywhere, and can surround virtually any set of circumstances.

I used to be terribly frightened to speak in public. The very thought of it made me want to faint, and on two occasions, I actually did! Then one day, everything changed. Suddenly I saw it differently, and I haven't been frightened since. I realized that people are people—we're all in this together, and I had nothing to fear. In reality, of course, there was no more or less to fear—all the factors were the same. After hoping for an insight for several years, I was fortunate enough to experience a mental shift in how I perceived public speaking. To this day, I see it differently. Again, it's all mental.

Be open to the possibility that you, too, might experience a sudden shift in some aspect of your relationship. Perhaps you've always argued about something and you'd like to put an end to that chapter in your life, peacefully, without effort. Or maybe you've fallen into the habit of taking your partner for granted, and it's time for an appreciation wakeup call. Whatever the circumstance, it's possible for you to have a sudden shift in the way you see it, an insight that will change your life for the better. Set the stage for a sudden insight and be on the lookout for what develops. You may be delighted at what occurs to you.

26.

AVOID THE "I'VE HAD A

REALLY HARD DAY" HABIT

One of our family's favorite songs is Shania Twain's "Honey, I'm Home." The kids, in particular, love to sing along in the backseat. In this upbeat, funny song, Twain sings about what a "hard day" she has had. She goes into tremendous detail about everything that went wrong. One thing after another. Everything that could have possibly gone wrong—did. Anyone who has ever had a horrible day can relate.

At the end of the song, you get a feeling of relief that her day is finally over. You can't help but make the connection between her detailed description of the negative events of the day and a feeling that all is now well.

While I'm the first to admit that there are times when a long complaining session feels really good—or when sharing about the difficult events of the day is necessary and cleansing—this is a very seductive and dangerous habit to get into, if you take it too far. It's easy for this type of daily review to become a way of life and to become a primary focus of conversation.

One of our best friends was dating a really nice woman. He was very fond of her in almost every way. She had one habit, however, that over time began to drive him crazy. Each night after work, they would either get together for dinner or talk on the phone. Her habit was to sing her own version of "Honey, I'm Home," but it wasn't funny. She had an interesting life and much to be grateful for, but her focus, almost all the time, was on whatever went wrong. And because plenty goes wrong for all of us, she never ran out of ammunition. The truth is, there isn't a correlation between reviewing negative events and a positive uplifted feeling. It's actually the other way around. Any positive feelings that exist between you and your partner exist *despite* the negative review of the day, not because of it.

Being extremely compassionate and a very good listener, our friend found it difficult to admit that he couldn't take it anymore. He noticed that he was beginning to forget that, in general, life is wonderful. They attempted to discuss the issue many times, but her position was that she was simply being honest about her feelings.

This can be a tricky habit to overcome because, like our friend's ex-girlfriend, we can almost always justify the "hard-day habit" with the facts of the day. It's important to remember, however, that there is usually far more to a typical day than those things that went wrong. In fact, you may have done twenty things during the course of the day, and nineteen probably went reasonably well—but you talk about the other one over dinner!

Again, no one is denying that life can be hard and that certain days are particularly difficult. Every once in a while, all of us need a listening ear, and upon occasion it's perfectly okay and healthy to vent. But try to avoid making the negative events of your day the primary topic of your evening conversation. When you nip this habit in the bud, you'll become aware of far more of what's good in life, and this joy will spread to your relationships. You'll end up being a lot more interesting to your partner, and so much more fun to be around.

27.

LET HIM BUY HIS LUNCH

Kris was talking with a woman about the challenge of sticking to a budget. The woman was telling Kris that she was furious and frustrated that her husband loved to go out to lunch, rather than allow her to make it for him. To her, this choice was an unnecessary extravagance, a waste of money that was jeopardizing their financial future. After all, she correctly pointed out, "He might spend seven or eight dollars going out, whereas I can make a delicious lunch for less than three."

Her husband's position was quite different. To him, going out to lunch was one of the few things he loved to do for himself, a luxury he felt he could easily afford. He felt under enormous pressure all day long at work, and getting away during his lunch hour to a quiet cafe or deli seemed to bring him peace of mind. It was something he looked forward to on a daily basis, and clearly, he wasn't going to give it up without a fight.

Obviously, this example could easily have been reversed. It's often the husband who is upset with his wife about her "extravagances." Certainly, we're not arguing against being frugal. In fact, in *Don't Worry, Make Money*, I argued for this woman's perspective as a great way to save money—which it certainly can be.

However, in this instance, this issue was causing great tension between them and was interfering with their love for one another. What should they do?

While financial circumstances would clearly contribute to the most appropriate answer, in this instance, it would be best for the woman to drop the issue and make the decision to share in her husband's joy. Whereas in many instances the difference of a few dollars a day would indeed make a significant difference in a couple's future financial security, that was not the case with this couple. Sure, the extra money would be nice—but at what cost? Is it more important to be "right" and demand that your partner see things your way—or is it more important to find simple ways to bring joy to your partner? What's more important—"future security" or "present-day harmony?" Again, we're not suggesting that you should sacrifice future security for present-day need fulfillment, but rather to learn to draw an appropriate line that takes into consideration the joys of your partner.

We couldn't resist writing about this subject because it's symbolic of something so much greater than the cost of lunch. The question is, "What is a simple pleasure that brings your partner joy really worth?" To us, the answer has always been, "It's worth a great deal." Whether you have to give up a little money, some time, a preference, or a little convenience, it's usually worth it to make a sacrifice in your partner's behalf. A genuinely contented partner contributes to a happy and satisfying relationship.

There is something magical that happens when you stop insisting on being "right," and instead soften your positions to accommodate your partner. Usually, the result is that your partner will also soften their position and, together, you'll find a way to gently compromise or find a solution that makes sense.

We're not suggesting that you always have to bend or accommodate your partner's needs, or that you should do so if the request is truly unreasonable. Yet, when you know that something isn't that big a deal, and it makes your partner happy, it might be better for your relationship if you allow your partner to have his or her way. Give it a try, and your relationship will prosper.

28.

SURPRISE HER WITH COMPLIMENTS

♥ Ten years ago I may not have included this strategy in a book because, to me, giving compliments is as natural as brushing my teeth. I've always enjoyed giving and receiving compliments, and I married one of the most generous compliment givers imaginable. However, after discussing this topic with hundreds of people, I've come to learn that, sadly, most don't receive nearly as many compliments as they would like, particularly from their partner.

There seem to be several reasons that people don't dish out very many compliments. First, many feel as though their partner doesn't need compliments. One of my own friends, for example, once told me, "Sara already knows that I love her cooking. She doesn't need me to tell her." Others simply forget how important it is. It's easy to take for granted those whom we are with a great deal of the time—so much so that their enormous contributions become invisible. I was talking to a man about his family. They had three school-age children, and for years, his wife had worked in all the kids' classrooms a minimum of once a week, usually more. He had never done this, even once. I was in awe as I said, "Wow, you must be grateful that your wife is so dedicated to your kids." It suddenly occurred to him how much work and dedication this took. He sheepishly admitted that he had never thought much about it—and had never once thanked his wife for her efforts. "Come to think of it," he added, "I've never thanked her for working so hard at her job, either."

Finally, some even associate the giving of compliments with a kind of weakness. The thinking is: If I were to give too many compliments, it might imply that I wasn't doing enough—or I wasn't good enough. A woman named Beth once told me that she didn't want to tell her husband she appreciated his attempts to help out around the house because "I do far more than he does, and if I give him a compliment, he'll think he's doing more than me."

Each of these reasons (and all the others) is seriously flawed. People need, thrive on, and appreciate compliments. We are also partially motivated by them. After all, if we don't know what our partner loves about us, it's far more difficult to please them. A teenage girl once told me at a book signing, "I know everything my boyfriend doesn't like about me, but very little about what he does like."

This is a simple strategy to implement. All you have to do is sense the importance of giving compliments, and begin doing so. As long as your compliments are genuine and from the heart, you can't lose. All you have to do is reflect on your partner and how much you have to be grateful for. What would you do without her, anyway? Wouldn't she love to hear that from you?

Let her know what you like about her. Tell her, not just once, but often. If you like something he does, let him know. If you appreciate the fact that your partner contributes to or is responsible for the family finances, let her know how you feel. If your husband or wife mows the lawn, don't take it for granted. Instead, yell out, "You're terrific. Thank you so much." The more you think about it, the more obvious it becomes and the easier it gets.

Never assume that a compliment isn't wanted or needed. This is one of those times when more really is better. Kris has probably told me 10,000 times how much she appreciates me for a variety of reasons. Because her words are genuine, it feels every bit as good as it did the first time she told me.

Take a few moments today and think about your partner. Think about all that he or she does to make your life better, easier, and more complete. Think about all of her talents and positive traits. The next time you see her or talk to her, surprise her with a compliment—and then make compliment giving a routine part of your life.

29.

STOP WISHING SHE (OR HE)
WERE DIFFERENT

There is no question that, philosophically, this is one of the most important strategies in this book. The connection between wishing our partner were different and our own level of dissatisfaction is powerful and significant. To make matters worse, this insidious habit is often invisible to ourselves, or at least very subtle.

When we love someone, it's tempting and perhaps almost inevitable to fall into the trap of yearning for a slightly "better" partner. This doesn't necessarily mean we actually want a different partner, only that we wish the partner we have was a little different from the way she actually is.

Whether we overtly acknowledge it or keep it to ourselves, almost everyone does this, however slightly. We might wish our partner were more like someone else, a better provider, more ambitious, gentler, a better listener, more passionate, better looking, less reactive, more helpful, or some combination of the above—but it's rare that it's not something.

The problem is, whenever there is a gap between what we have and what we want, we will feel dissatisfied or in some way frustrated. It's a hard-and-fast rule of life that applies to our relationships, just as it does to all other aspects of our lives. It's difficult, however, to make this connection because it seems, on the surface, that your lack of satisfaction is coming directly from your partner. The almost universal conclusion becomes, "If only my partner were different, or would shape up in some way, or change to meet my expectations, I would then be happy."

What most of us do in response to this seemingly logical conclusion is to yearn, fantasize, wish, hope for, or in some cases demand that our partner change. "By golly," we tell ourselves, "I'm not going to be happy until they do."

The result is that when our partner fails to change or to meet our expectations, we remain dissatisfied. We may even feel slighted or resentful because we are convinced that it is our partner who is preventing us from being happy. It's their fault. I could easily convince myself, "If only Kris would be more like I want her to be, I'd be happier," just as Kris could convince herself of the same thing about me. Either way, it's absolutely guaranteed that whichever of us continues to believe this to be the case will remain in some way dissatisfied. It's as predictable as the sun rising in the morning.

Unfortunately, even in those rare instances when our partner does change, any satisfaction we experience will be short-lived. When we attach our own happiness to the insistence that our partner change, it's only a matter of time before we need additional changes. I've met dozens of people—men and women—who desperately wanted their partner to become more helpful around the home. When their "dream" came true, either through conflict, compromise, or an honest effort by their partner, they quickly discovered that the changes weren't extensive enough. More changes would be better.

The trick is to see (and feel) the connection between the act of wishing that your partner were different from the way he or she actually is—and the corresponding and predictable feeling that something is missing, or not quite right. Once you see this dynamic connection between your own thoughts and the way you feel, you're in for an enormous surprise. In fact, your relationship will never be the same again.

As an experiment, take note of your dissatisfactions, the aspects of your partner that you wish were different. Now ask yourself the questions, "What would happen if I could stop wishing she needed to change to be complete in my eyes?" "What would happen if I decided to love her just the way she is?" Look for ways to love her as she is, right now.

When your attention shifts in this way, the changes in yourself will be noticeable and dramatic. Your demands will soften, and your dissatisfactions will begin to disappear. You'll become more accepting and forgiving, as well as substantially less judgmental. Your ability to communicate nondefensively will be enhanced, as will your ability to bring out the best in your partner. Finally, the love you feel will be more genuine and unconditional. The love you've been waiting to experience is within your own grasp. All you have to do is stop wishing she were different.

30.

DON'T PUT YOUR PARTNER
ON THE SPOT

Right up there near the top of the "I can't stand it when my partner does that" list is the nerve-wracking, insulting, and oh-so-irritating habit of putting your partner on the spot. Or, put another way, this means forcing your partner to make an instant decision at an awkward moment, when if he were to choose a certain answer, it would make him look bad.

Here is a classic example: The phone rings. You're not in the mood to talk, so your partner answers the phone. On the other end is a mutual friend who is calling to ask if the two of you would like to get together over the weekend.

For weeks, you've been looking forward to a quiet weekend and a chance to catch up on some home projects. Your partner, however, is in a social mood and rejoices at the thought of getting together.

Here's where it gets sticky. Your partner pulls the phone away from her ear and says to you, "Honey, I'm so excited. It's Susan. We're all going to get together this weekend. Doesn't that sound great?" Susan, on the other end of the line, can hear everything you're saying and is now anxiously awaiting your response.

If ever there was an uncomfortable moment, this is it. What are you supposed to do? In all honesty, you really don't want to get together with Susan.

However, she's a really good friend and you haven't seen her in quite a while. Furthermore, she's excited to see you—and your partner is excited too.

But now you're on the spot. You don't have even a single moment to reflect on your priorities or on how much time you need this weekend to get your other things done. You don't know all the facts or even exactly what you're being asked to do. If you're completely honest, you might appear selfish, hurt your friend's feelings, or upset your partner. If, on the other hand, you agree, despite not really wanting to go, you are probably going to feel a little ripped off, perhaps even resentful. At that point, the best you can do is balance your options the best that you can and try to remember that this, too, is small stuff. Either decision will be okay.

However, there is a solution so simple and respectful that it's a shame not to use it. Philosophically, it might be called, "It's not fair to put my partner on the spot."

To implement this philosophy, all your partner would have had to do is to honestly express her own enthusiasm to meet with your friend. Then, she would politely say, "I can't speak for (you), but I sure hope he will be able to come along too. I'll ask him if he has any plans and get back to you right away. I can't wait to see you."

That's it. Problem solved. Everyone wins, no one's feelings are hurt, and no one is put on the spot. You now have the chance to think about your options, hear how important your involvement is to your partner, sort out all the factors, and make a decision. What could be easier than that?

Perhaps the most awkward way to be put on the spot is in front of other people. This is even worse than the example of the phone because, in these cases, others not only hear you but can see you, too—your gestures, body language, and so forth. You can put your partner on the spot in many ways.

Unfortunately, none of them are experienced or received in a loving or appreciative way. Instead, being put on the spot usually elicits a defensive or some other type of negative reaction. In any event, it almost always creates a stressful environment.

One of the easiest ways to avoid sweating the small stuff in love is not to be unnecessarily put to the test. And if you don't want to put your partner to the test, this one is a no-brainer! Not always, but usually, you can avoid putting your partner on the spot. If you do, you'll be rewarded with a more relaxed and probably more loving partner.

31.

THINK BEFORE YOU SPEAK

We have a dear friend who shared with us the following story: She had just returned home from a long bike ride with some friends. She was really excited because the time it took to complete the second half of the ride was less than the time it took to complete the first half. Because she was trying really hard to get into better physical condition, she felt this was truly significant and she was justifiably proud of herself. Excitedly, as she walked in the front door, she shared her success with her husband. Without thinking, he blurted out, "The reason you were able to go faster on the way back is because there is more downhill."

Ouch! Our friend felt as if someone had stabbed her in the back. Her story had been minimized, and she felt as if she had been "put in her place."

Obviously, people have said far worse things, and I'm sure she was able to get over his thoughtless comment within a relatively short period of time. The question, however, is, "Why did he have to say it?" Whether he was technically correct or not is irrelevant. There was absolutely no possibility that anything positive could come of his comment. Nothing was added. The only possible end results were hurt feelings, a lowering of self-esteem, and a dose of resentment. Why would anyone do something with such a predictable negative result? Yet, people do it all the time—and usually to the person they love the most.

What's interesting is that our friend's husband is a genuinely nice person. It's highly unlikely that he meant any harm, and he truly loves his wife. His fatal flaw here wasn't a lack of love—but lack of the discipline to think before he spoke.

This tendency to speak without thinking comes out in many ways—sarcasm, putdowns, one-upping, correcting, or simply saying something unnecessary, but in some way mean. It usually happens when you're in a reactive state of mind such as when you're a little tired, overwhelmed, stressed, or frustrated. How often have you blurted something out while you were in a really bad mood, only to regret it later?

A general rule of thumb is this: If you have even the slightest doubt about whether or not your upcoming response is appropriate, ask yourself the following two-part question: "Is my next comment going to add to this conversation—is it going to bring us closer, or is it likely to drive us apart?" Asking this very simple question will eliminate a vast majority of unnecessary hurts that would otherwise be inflicted on your partner. It's important to remember, too, that a hurtful comment inspired by a lack of thinking doesn't exist in a vacuum. You can imagine that when a person is a victim of an unnecessary hurtful comment, she will usually become at least a little defensive and will probably have a few things to say in response. Invariably, this turns into an argument or some other type of dysfunctional and nonloving interaction. Had our friend's husband, for example, taken even one second to pay attention to his thoughts before he spoke, he surely would have chosen to say something different—or perhaps nothing at all. Then, instead of hurt feelings and a day of resentment, their time together could have been spent enjoying each other's company.

This strategy is short and sweet. You can think of it as a "heads up," or a simple reminder of something that's obvious on the surface but sometimes easy to forget: It's really important that we pause for a moment when our partner is finished speaking so that we can, in turn, think before we speak. This is more validation that the essence of having a loving relationship isn't very complicated. What seems to be most important is that we try to be thoughtful and kind, and that we stay out of our own way, at least most of the time.

32.

DISCOVER WHAT PART
YOU ARE PLAYING

♥ There are many characteristics that separate truly great relationships from all the others—a loving heart, thoughtfulness, generosity, a lack of jealousy, kindness, shared values, trust, integrity, to name just a few.

Here is another characteristic, however, to add to this illustrious list that is equally important, yet discussed and acknowledged far less often: the willingness and desire to acknowledge your own contributions to your problems. This willingness is so powerful that, combined with a loving heart, you'd be in pretty good shape if you did little else right.

Think about it for a moment. How often do you hear someone say, "Gee, I can really see how I'm contributing to this issue"? I chuckle when I ask the question because the answer is, "Almost never." What we usually hear instead are comments designed to blame someone else for the problems in our lives and in our relationships. We hear statements like "My partner is too demanding," "He doesn't listen to me," "She is too emotional," "He doesn't do his part," as well as hundreds of other "It's not my fault" statements and complaints. Unfortunately, this tendency is useless and counterproductive at best—and extremely destructive at worst.

Be honest. Have you ever, even once, heard someone respond to a blaming statement with a positive response? For example, if you say in a blaming or bitter tone, "You're always picking on me," can you even imagine your partner saying, "You're right, honey, I am. Thank you for sharing that with me. I'm going to start working on that tendency right away. I love you so much"?

Not a chance. Instead, you're likely to get a defensive response—or no response at all, but lots of quiet resentment. In this example, your partner will see you as being unreasonable, as if you're sweating the small stuff!

It's entirely different, however, when you strive to see your own contribution to any issues you might be having. Instead of tuning you out or resisting what you have to say, your partner is far more likely to perk up and really listen to your thoughts.

For example, you might reflect on your own tendency to feel "picked on." You could then say to your partner, "I'm beginning to realize that I have a tendency to get a bit sensitive. It bugs me that I feel picked on by you so much of the time. I'm certainly going to work on it, but what do you think is going on?"

Your willingness to reflect on your own contribution, and your nondefensive attitude, will set forth a positive emotional climate and open the door to a growth-oriented discussion. Your partner is far more likely to see your point and to reflect on your feelings. Maybe he does pick on you too much. Perhaps he didn't know how you felt. Or, who knows? Maybe you *are* a little too sensitive.

You will identify solutions in a fraction of the time when you strive to see your part. Obviously this doesn't mean your partner is perfect, or that there aren't things he could be doing differently, or habits he could change, or that, even occasionally, it *never* is all his fault.

It's not always the case, but usually there are two sides to the issue—both parties contributing in some way to a problem. When neither partner sees their own part, change is difficult, unlikely, or even impossible. However, when either partner sees his or her contribution to a problem, a reasonable solution will usually surface. Give this strategy some thought and your relationship will seem less confusing in no time.

33.

FINISH THE JOB

Rachel had been looking forward to going out with her friends, who were coming in from out of town, for several months. Finding the perfect time was difficult because of coordinating all the schedules that were involved, particularly since she worked part time and had three children. The only evening that worked for the group was a "back-to-school night" with the kids, so a babysitter was out of the question. Either she or her husband Rick had to be there.

Rick, a conscious and loving father, works full time, and then some. When the evening finally arrived, Rachel was very grateful to Rick for being home with the kids. He had, after all, been forced to cancel an appointment and miss out on an exciting business venture so that he could be there—so that she could go out.

Rachel had a great time reconnecting with her friends. Her heart sank, however, the moment she walked in the door. Everyone including Rick was already asleep, but the house looked like a bomb had gone off. Immediately, she felt as if going out with her friends had been a mistake. Rather than being able to go to bed refreshed, she became angry that she had to come home and start cleaning up messes she had nothing to do with.

This is a sad story because, in fairness, Rick had gone to some lengths to be there. He was tired and needed some rest. However, his lack of effort—

his unwillingness to finish the job—turned what would have been a wonderful and relaxing evening into a pain in the rear end for Rachel! An event she had looked forward to for several months was overshadowed by the hassle of coming home to a disaster.

In this story, "finishing the job" would have meant taking half an hour or so to make a reasonable effort in picking up the house. But it just as easily could have been making the phone calls that you promised you would make, delivering on a promise, or following through on any number of other commitments or chores that would make life a tiny bit easier for your partner. It's really that simple.

Needless to say, there are plenty of exceptions to this rule. There are times when you just can't do things—you're either too exhausted or too busy, or you just plain forgot. As a general rule of thumb, however, the moral of the story is this: Whenever possible and within reason, try to go the extra mile for your partner. Do whatever is necessary to finish the job. That way, your partner won't have to sweat the small stuff—because you will already have done so!

34.

THINK GENTLE THOUGHTS

Being a generally optimistic person, I've always assumed that thinking positive thoughts was a major key to happiness. And while I still assume this to be the case, I've learned that perhaps even more powerful than thinking positive thoughts is learning to think gently. I'm certain that if your goal is to have a loving relationship where little things don't interfere with that love, this is a strategy worth taking seriously.

An interesting exercise is to fill your mind with gentle, loving thoughts and then try to get irritated. My guess is that you won't be able to do it! The problem is, the qualities of a gentle mind are inconsistent with annoyance—the two are mutually exclusive. When your mind is gentle, your responses to ordinary events—especially small stuff—will tend to be compassionate. Usually, you'll be able to keep your sense of humor as well as your perspective. Rather than reacting harshly to the events of the day, you'll respond from a place of kindness. Simply put, the normal things that happen during the course of a day won't bug you quite as much and won't seem like such a big deal.

Gentle thoughts are those that reinforce the beauty of life and the privilege of being here. They range from thoughts of love and peace to those of forgiveness and generosity. They often include a hint of gratitude.

I've seen this ever-so-simple strategy positively affect even the most serious of people. I remember working with a man who epitomized the "Type A" personality. He was driven, hardworking, demanding, and really uptight. His marriage was in trouble because his expectations were as high for his wife and kids as they were for his employees. In his mind, there was no room for error. Everything had to be perfect. Otherwise, he would express his disapproval in unsightly ways.

I asked him to humor me by agreeing to try an experiment. Because he was obsessed with "being the best" at whatever he set out to do, I had no doubt that he would give it his best effort. I told him that, for an entire day, I wanted him to fill his mind with nothing but gentle thoughts. Each time his mind drifted toward achievement, perfection, winning, and whatever else, he was to bring his mind back to more gentle thinking. Those were my instructions.

With a mind focused on being gentle, he couldn't help but give his family a little more slack. His expectations softened, enough for his wife to notice. He was slightly more patient and a little less irritable. Most noticeable to his kids was that he was in less of a hurry—he actually sat with them at dinner without glancing at his watch. Even though the changes were small, they were enough for him to take notice. It was an eye-opening experience for him to notice that his wife and children were less stressed out around him.

Despite his living an extremely complicated life and dealing with very complex issues, this simple little strategy was the one that ultimately opened the door to some positive changes. Obviously it took a great deal of time and lots of practice to erase his old tendencies—one day didn't do it all. However, his willingness to experiment with gentle thinking may have saved his marriage and, at very least, showed him some important dynamics about what it means to be in a relationship. Sometimes the simplest ideas are the most powerful.

35.

STAY COMPASSIONATE

♥ When two people fall in love, they often become the center of each other's lives. They listen to and respect one another, and above all, they are compassionate. When one isn't feeling well, the other is by their side; when one is hurt—physically or emotionally—they share in the pain of their partner. They want to hear about each other's days and the experiences that have shaped their lives. They do so, not out of obligation, but out of love. It's seen as a privilege and a source of joy to hear each other's stories, to learn from one another and to share their experiences.

Compassion is defined as a sympathetic feeling. To be compassionate means you strive to know what it's like to be in the shoes of another person. Generally, we feel compassion when we see someone suffering; we want to reach out to them—to be a source of support, help, love, or understanding. Compassion is one of the beautiful characteristics that make us human. The more compassion we feel and express, the more human we become.

There is something strange, however, that seems to occur in most relationships—especially long-term ones. Gradually, over time, we lose our compassion for our partner. Somehow, we begin to see them in a different light than we do others—we take them for granted and forget, or lose sight of, the fact that our partner is human, too, and is subject to the same pain and suffering as everyone else. The point is, while it's relatively easy to experience compassion for a complete stranger who might be hungry, sick, injured, or experiencing grief or loss, we fail to open our hearts in the same way to the person we love most in the world—particularly when the pain is regarding day-to-day "stuff."

If you haven't yet lost your feelings of compassion for your partner—don't. Stay compassionate, and your relationship will be on solid, loving ground. If you have lost your compassion, however, or if it's slipping away, you can get it back. All it takes is a simple reminder that your partner's pain is every bit as real as anyone else's. He or she is subject to the same fears, feelings, doubts, and concerns as everyone else. When she is frightened or hurt, her need for a loving hug and someone to talk to is equally as legitimate as yours and mine. When she's had a really hard day, her need to talk about it makes absolute sense and shouldn't in any way be minimized. Keep in mind that when your partner is angry or frustrated—even when they are expressing their feelings toward you—the last thing they need is a negative or defensive reaction from you. What they probably need is your love and compassion, they need for you to reach out to them and open your heart. And when you do, you'll be amazed at how often little problems and issues of the day dissolve and go away. Daily compassion strengthens your love and mutual respect for one another like nothing else. It's comforting to know that someone understands—especially you. If you can maintain and deepen the compassion you have for your partner, you will probably end up with a rich and nourishing relationship.

It's also important to be compassionate to yourself; to remember that you, too, are human. When you mess up, make a mistake, say something wrong, lose your bearings or simply have a really bad day—be kind to yourself. Give yourself a break. Soften your reactions by reminding yourself that you can only do the best that you can. By offering yourself love and patience rather than harsh judgment, you are able to become the best person you can be in every sense of the word.

36.

JUMP-START
YOUR RELATIONSHIP

There's a widespread belief that the time to turn to experts is when your relationship is in trouble. After all, there's no question that a good psychologist, minister, priest, rabbi, social worker, marriage counselor, or other qualified professional can be enormously helpful during difficult times.

However, it's also the case that these as well as many other (including less traditional) professionals can be effectively used to jump-start your relationship, to push or encourage you toward growth, better communication, and increased love for one another.

Many relationships, even good ones, can become static or habitual. It's easy to begin taking each other for granted or to lose that wonderful spark that existed in times gone by. This doesn't mean there's anything wrong with your relationship; only that it could be even better. Often, a tiny shift in your thinking, a change of attitude, a dose of perspective, or a few new tips can make a world of difference.

I used to teach courses on happiness, which included, among other things, tips such as the ones you read about in my books. Often, couples would attend, not because there was anything wrong with their relationship, but because they wanted a little jump-start. One of my greatest compliments was when people would say, "That was just what we needed." What they learned was always very simple, just a little reminder of what it takes to be a happy person or a happy couple.

You can get the same kind of positive jolt by taking a class together on good communication skills or a workshop on becoming a more loving partner, or even sitting together for an hour-long lecture by one of your favorite authors or speakers. Many bookstores have free events where authors will speak for a while, followed by a book signing. There are audiotapes on relationship skills you can purchase, then create some quiet time to listen to them together. If you prefer, you can read to each other out of a book that inspires you to become closer. Even something this simple can provide the jump start you're looking for. The act of doing one or more of these things is an acknowledgment to one another that your relationship is important, a statement that you want to continue to grow together.

We encourage you to start looking around for new ways to jump-start your relationship. It's a great way to spend time together and is almost always a great deal of fun.

37.

DON'T ALLOW PASSING THOUGHTS
TO TURN INTO ISSUES

I could make a case that, in terms of learning to stop sweating the small stuff in your relationships, you'd be in pretty good shape if you mastered nothing other than this single strategy. It's that powerful and important!

Thousands of thoughts pass through our minds each and every day. These thoughts are made up of our ideas, plans, expectations, and memories, among other things. Some of our thoughts are happy; many are not. We have worries, concerns, hopes, predictions, and for most of us, plenty of confusion. We think about the past and we think about the future.

As thoughts pass through your mind, essentially one of two things can happen. First, your thought can be a passing thought. Most of our thoughts fall into this category. We have so many thoughts throughout the day that it would be impossible, impractical, and extremely confusing to examine each one.

For example, while driving, I might think to myself, "I wonder if Kris remembered to respond to our dinner invitation." If I don't take it too seriously and I allow it to pass by, it's gone as quickly as it arrived. If it seems relevant, I might make a note to call her later in the day to remind her. If not, I'll probably forget it altogether—or it will come to mind again, at some later time. Then, the next thought pops into my mind.

The other possibility is that I hold that thought in my mind, as if to examine it. I keep it right there "in my face" where I can study it. I give it my undivided attention and attach significance to it. While it's there in my mind, I might think of examples where Kris was forgetful, times when she assured me that she was going to make a phone call on our behalf, but she didn't get around to it. Within a matter of seconds, I'm a little irritated. Notice that Kris isn't even in the car with me—but I'm getting more frustrated at her by the second.

You can probably sense how easy it can be to create an issue over practically anything. All that's really required is that you continue feeding the thought with your attention. You might speculate that the "forgetfulness" impacts other parts of your relationship, or that there is something wrong with your partner. The problem is, if you don't see how your own thinking contributes to the issues that frustrate you, then pretty soon your relationship will be filled up with various issues—and it's always going to seem like it's your partner's fault.

On the surface, you might think it's a little funny that something so minor could negatively impact a relationship. And, in a way, it is. The truth is, however, that while the details are different, this process is extremely common, and to one degree or another, it happens to all of us.

It's important to note that a person might be in a relationship with someone who is far more forgetful than Kris, yet he doesn't allow it to bother him. While he doesn't pretend that his partner isn't ever forgetful, and while he would prefer that she become less so, he nevertheless doesn't allow his own thoughts to spiral out of control. Instead, he finds a healthy way to deal with it.

The solution is to be willing to accept the fact that many annoyances are simply passing thoughts that we are taking a little too seriously. The next time you find yourself feeling irritated, check in with your thinking. See whether you might be holding onto something instead of simply dropping it or letting it pass by. If you do, you'll find that most issues in your relationship will begin to fade away. Of course, if something is truly important, it will most certainly return. In the meantime, instead of struggling with such problems, consider letting them go so that you can spend your energy enjoying each other.

38.

BECOME A
LOW-MAINTENANCE PARTNER

♥ Most people report that they have experienced two distinct types of houseguests. The first might be called "high maintenance." These are guests who show up and take over your life. They require lots of attention, use your car, and need to be constantly entertained. If not, they act bored. When they use the phone, they forget to use their credit card. They dominate your time and require that you spend virtually every minute together, including all meals. While they are visiting, you find yourself craving space and solitude. They show no signs of independence and act disappointed when you have things you must attend to. Even though you may love them, you find yourself dreading their arrival and, once they do arrive, you count the days until they leave.

The other type of houseguest can be called "low maintenance." These guests are delightful. You spend plenty of time together, laughing and sharing, yet, in some ways you don't even know they are there. They are no trouble whatsoever. They make it perfectly clear that they don't need to be entertained, even for a moment. In fact, they let you know they have plenty to do. They treasure the time they spend with you, but don't expect a great deal of it. In a word, they are effortless.

A very similar distinction can be made in more intimate relationships. On one end of the spectrum are the high-maintenance people. These individuals are usually demanding and needy, requiring lots of attention. They are upset a great deal of the time and they usually let you know about it. They need to be entertained and looked after. They are often jealous and insecure. So, when you have other things to attend to or when you don't have time to spend with them, they require an explanation. These people are "on your back" or nagging a great deal of the time. They lack real independence. They might be nice people, but they are a great deal of work.

On the other end of the spectrum are the lowest-maintenance people. These are individuals who are easy to be with, in every sense of the word. They are seldom needy or demanding and are sensitive to the fact that, as important as they know they are to their partner, they are not the center of the universe. They are highly independent and sensitive to the fact that most people need some space. They are open and love to share, but don't spend an inordinate amount of time complaining about the wrongs of the world. They cherish their time with their partner but are understanding when it is not possible to be together.

Most of us, of course, fall somewhere in between. Probably no one is completely maintenance-free, and luckily, very few people are at the other extreme, either. Yet, when you remind yourself of the lightness of the lower side of the scale and the heaviness and effort that are associated with the higher side, it becomes pretty obvious that you increase the odds of having a fun and loving relationship if you can become a lower-maintenance person than you already are.

We all know that life can be tough. Ideally, our relationship is one part of life that feels like a sanctuary—a partnership that is mutually nourishing and enriching both spiritually and emotionally. A good relationship makes your life a little easier, not more complicated and filled up with demands and the need to be constantly explaining yourself.

Again, it's inevitable that some of the qualities of a high-maintenance person are going to show up from time to time in every relationship—it certainly does in ours. No big deal! It's not the occasional neediness, insecurity, or nagging that will interfere with the quality of your relationship, but rather the ongoing pattern that becomes burdensome to deal with. So, take an honest look. Wherever you happen to fall on the scale is perfectly fine. We predict, however, that if you make some minor changes, however small, your partner will begin to notice and appreciate them. We think you'll find that it will be easier and less stressful (on both of you) if you can become a low-maintenance partner.

39.

DO IT YOUR WAY

♥ Obviously, every relationship is unique. We're all different. Each of us brings to our relationships our own history, plans, fears, dreams, disappointments, and expectations. We're attracted and drawn to different things and are bugged by certain others. We've all had at least some painful experiences that shape our personality and, hopefully, many happy ones as well. Different things push our buttons.

Yet, despite the fact that each relationship is molded differently, many of us have the tendency to act as if our relationship needs to fit into a certain mold, that we have to be like everyone else. This is unfortunate because doing so can create a barrier between what you know is true for you and how you choose to live your life. It can also prevent you from following your own bliss and from discovering great joy and depth in your life together. It can adversely affect your relationship in many ways—from the very mundane (e.g., encouraging you to attend parties you don't really want to go to) to the very serious (e.g., what church you feel you must attend to keep peace in the family).

A consistent observation we've made is that happy, unfrustrated couples tend to do things their own way and make up their own set of rules. Instead of looking over their shoulders to see if they are getting approval from others—friends, neighbors, family members—they discover for themselves what brings them joy, and they live their lives their own way. Ultimately, this makes them happier and more inwardly peaceful individually and as a couple. A respect for differences and different ways of doing things also creates a more respectful attitude toward others. This, in turn, helps deepen an attitude of compassion and love for all of humanity.

The two of us have always done things a little differently from many couples we love and respect. For example, we share responsibilities at home and with our children, rather than being locked into specific roles. Although almost none of our friends do so, on occasion, we enjoy taking separate vacations. We have friends of the opposite sex without feeling jealous, something many of our friends don't understand. We don't feel guilty leaving our kids with great sitters so that we can enjoy each other's company, a philosophy quite different from many wonderful parents including some in our own families. We are committed to our own spiritual path, which differs slightly from many people we love.

We have found that, despite the fact that at times others either don't understand or may even attempt to manipulate us through guilt to change or do things differently, we know we are better off doing things our own way. We can certainly learn from others and are always open to changing the ways we do things if there is a better way—but not simply because we don't feel we fit in, or that someone is disappointed in us. Our commitment is to be kind, gentle, and loving to each other and to the people in our world. And while we certainly fall short of our ideals at times, we have decided that, ultimately, only *we* can decide how to make that happen.

Because we believe that we need to do things our own way, we also find it extremely easy to honor the ways of others. This makes it easy for us to be friends with all types of people and to respect and enjoy our differences. This keeps our conflicts to a minimum and our frustration under control.

This same philosophy applies to us as a couple. Although we're partners for life and share many similar traits, we do many things very differently and have many different preferences. And because that's okay with us, it keeps us from being upset, irritated, bothered, or annoyed with each other simply because we're different.

It's easy to get caught in the trap of comparing your relationship to that of others or to think about whether you're meeting their expectations or not. A joyful relationship, however, is one that you create—and that is uniquely yours. We hope you'll honor your own way and discover what works best for you.

40.

WAKE UP AND THINK ABOUT THREE THINGS YOU LOVE ABOUT HER

♥ At the risk of sounding corny, this strategy really works. I've found that it's nearly impossible to get too uptight or to sweat the small stuff with your partner when you have recently reminded yourself about why you love her so much. This holds true whether you're dating and live in different cities, or married and living together.

I'll give you a personal example that demonstrates how practical this really is. A few days ago I woke up and thought about the way Kris brightens the lives of others with her beautiful smile. For as long as I can remember, she's been smiling and being nice to everyone, even strangers. I don't think I've ever picked her up at the airport when she didn't have a new friend she had met on the plane! This led me to my second loving thought about her: I remembered how many times I've been upset about something and she eased my mind by reminding me, "It's just small stuff." More than most people, she has a way of not getting too uptight about little things. My final thought before getting out of bed was related to an activity one of our kids was doing later that day. Specifically, my thought was, "I'm sure glad Kris is willing and able to get the girls ready for these types of things." I almost laughed out loud as I thought about how different our two daughters' hair and clothing would appear if I were in charge.

So there you have it—three of the many things I love about Kris. The entire process probably took about a minute or two, but it set the stage for the rest of the day. Here's what I mean.

I walked outside to get the newspaper and noticed that Kris had left the door to her car unlocked with her purse and keys on the front seat, one of my major pet peeves. She's so trusting that she doesn't always think about security. But here's where it gets interesting. Because my mind was fresh with loving thoughts about Kris, I sort of rolled my eyes and shrugged it off. No big deal—no reason to fret. I barely gave it a second thought. It wasn't that I tried not to give it a second thought—it just didn't have any sting.

The rest of the story is speculation, but I'll give you an educated guess as to what might have happened had my thoughts taken a different direction. The question is, What *would* have been my reaction to the unlocked door had I awakened and failed to think about such positive things? Or, worse yet: What would have happened had I awakened and immediately began to fill my mind—as many do—with my many responsibilities, to the point of putting myself in a stressful mind-set? It's almost a rhetorical question. The answer is obvious—I would have become upset and irritated.

This doesn't mean that if you think about several things you love about your partner, first thing every morning, that you're never again going to become irritated or annoyed. It will, however, substantially reduce the likelihood of this occurring. And even when you do get bothered, it won't be as severe. This strategy is quick, simple, effective, and virtually effortless. What's more, it feels good. You'll be amazed at how easy it will be to stop sweating the small stuff in love!

41.

CHOOSE PEACE
OVER IRRITATION

To this day, I'm often surprised and delighted at the effectiveness of this simple yet powerful strategy. Each time I remember that I have this choice, I'm rewarded with less irritation and frustration, as well as additional moments of relationship harmony.

Every moment, it's as if we're at an emotional fork in the road. Something happens, followed by our choice either to react or to respond. Unfortunately, because we usually react so quickly and habitually, it often doesn't seem as though we have a choice. Our reactions seem to have a life of their own and occur almost instantly, seemingly out of our control. It seems appropriate to act and feel irritated when something happens that you don't like.

But when you look more carefully, you'll notice that you really do have a choice. Rather than reacting as you always do, you have the power and the ability to respond differently. And this is very important because, in the absence of your willingness to make this choice, you'll be frustrated each time your partner proves to be less than perfect.

A friend of mine told me the following story: He had agreed to meet his wife at a department store to do some shopping. This was her idea, not his. Furthermore, he had juggled his day to accommodate her schedule.

The problem was, although he was on time, she wasn't. He had been waiting almost half an hour and was beginning to "see red." His mind began to fill with all kinds of negativity—judgments, anger, disappointment, and stress. He began to remember other times she had done something similar. He was getting really irritated.

Then it hit him, as if out the blue. He realized he could continue to fill his mind with negativity and irritation as he had done so many times in the past—or he could choose peace instead. In that moment, it all seemed very simple. It was true that his wife was late, but the irritation was within his own head. *He* was the one who was suffering. He reminded himself that his own peace and sanity, as well as the quality of his marriage, were far more important than filling his mind with anger and continuing to justify why he "had a right to be angry." He let go of his irritated thoughts and decided to look around the store, and to wait patiently. He decided not to sweat the small stuff.

Within a few minutes his wife entered the story in a mad rush. She fully expected him to be angry and to give her an annoying lecture. She was shocked at his genuinely calm demeanor. He had chosen peace instead of irritation. Instead of being angry, he was compassionate. Because he was so authentically nondefensive, she apologized and assured him that she was embarrassed to have kept him waiting for so long. Her apology was sincere.

What could easily have turned into a bitter power struggle turned out to be a peaceful afternoon of togetherness and a positive reinforcement of the importance of their relationship. He felt empowered, knowing that he made a loving, peaceful choice instead of succumbing to his normal reactions—and she felt enormous respect and gratitude for her husband's willingness to let go of her mistake. Because of his choice, the experience brought them closer together.

This same choice exists in virtually any situation. Dozens of times a day, things either go wrong or life turns out to be some way other than you would like it to be in that moment. And whether it's your partner acting in a way that you don't like or something else altogether, it's yet another chance for you to practice letting it go, a chance to choose peace over irritation. This doesn't mean you're condoning bad behavior or that you don't care when things go wrong. It simply means that you've decided that being peaceful is the best way of being. There's no question that if you make this choice as often as possible, both you as an individual and your relationship will benefit greatly.

42.

DON'T SWEAT
THE OCCASIONAL CRITICISM

Sometimes, when someone is criticized, you'd think by the reaction that we were in the midst of a national crisis! Many people get so upset when they are criticized—especially by their partner—that they not only get defensive and overreact, but they strike back, or even fall apart. If you look at criticism realistically, however, and with a bit of perspective, we think you'll agree that it's really not that big a deal.

The truth is, none of us is exempt from the rest of the human race. We're all going to get our fair share of criticism during our lifetime. And, if we're in a relationship, at least some of that criticism is going to come from our partner. It's inevitable because our partner spends a great deal of time with us. They see us at our best and at our worst. They know (and regularly witness) our weaknesses as well as our strengths. At times, we're around our partner when we are in really low moods and most susceptible to feeling criticized. If we're honest, we'll probably admit that this is the time we are most likely to criticize, as well.

In addition, we're around our partner during those times when they are in a low mood, when they are most likely to dish out some criticism. Let's face it. Our partner knows how to push our buttons and it's human nature to push them every once in a while when you're in a low mood. So, it's unrealistic—in fact, probably a little unfair—to expect that your partner won't, at times, criticize you. It's just part of being in a relationship.

When someone criticizes you, it doesn't mean they don't love you. Nor does it mean they don't respect or admire you. Criticism is just something that people do for a variety of reasons. Sometimes we criticize out of habit; other times it's because we're frustrated, confused, stressed-out, or insecure. Occasionally, we even criticize because we see a flaw that really does need to be fixed. In other words, not all criticism is unjustified. Often, it's actually constructive, even helpful.

The best way to deal with occasional criticism is to make allowances for it, and accept the fact that it is going to be directed at you from time to time. In a way, you have to expect it. It's similar to rain. You know it's going to come; you just don't know exactly when, and under what circumstances. And just like you wouldn't get mad at rain—you simply put up an umbrella and accept it—you don't need to be concerned about small amounts of criticism. All you need to do is allow it to be there—accept it, and let it go.

Often when you take this more philosophical stance and don't get so defensive when you're criticized, it seems to occur far less often and, when it does, it seems to fade much more quickly. For whatever reason, criticism feeds on defensiveness. When you react, it's as if the person doing the criticizing feels as though the criticism was justified and the need to criticize continues. On the other hand, when you let it go without ruffling your feathers too much, the urge and need to criticize fade into the distance.

Gale told me that her husband was usually a really nice guy but that he was sometimes critical of what he called her "lack of understanding of technology." Apparently, he loved to work with computers and couldn't understand why it was so difficult for her. I asked her how often his criticism was expressed and she said, "Probably three or four times a month." I asked her how she typically would deal with his comments. She said that she would usually become a little defensive and hurt. She also assured me that she had discussed the issue with her husband on many occasions, but that he just wouldn't stop.

I shared with her the essence of this strategy and she admitted that although she had never considered such a "passive" approach, she saw the logic and would certainly give it a try.

About a month later I received a really nice message from her saying that learning to deflect her husband's criticism was one of the easiest things she had ever done. She had decided to "reframe" his comments so that, each time he would begin his criticism, she would remind herself that what he really meant was that he cared about her and wanted her to benefit from the ease of technology. Rather than resisting his words, fighting back, and giving him something to hang onto, she would simply agree and say something like, "You're so right dear—I really should learn." Her lack of reaction was so unheated that he would drop it in a second. At some point he threw up his hands and said with a chuckle, "What's the use?"

Gale had turned her husband's criticism into a game. And she was learning to win! That's it, no big deal. There were no fancy techniques or heavy psychological issues to discuss or memorize—just a little perspective, a willingness to see the innocence in his criticism and to have a bit of a sense of humor. While there's no way to prove it, my guess is that had she continued with her defensive, take-it-really-seriously reaction, the criticism would still be there. As it turned out, it quickly disappeared.

Even if your partner's criticism is more serious or happens more often, this strategy should ease the pain. Without your reaction, there will be less energy to feed the criticism. Take it less seriously and it will begin to fade away.

43.

STAY PLAYFUL

One of the most satisfying compliments I ever remember the two of us, as a couple, receiving was from someone whom we have never even met. We were sitting in a movie theater waiting for the previews to begin. We were whispering, joking around, laughing, giggling, and just having a great time.

I overheard the woman behind us whisper to her husband, "Look at those two, probably out on one of their first dates. Do you remember what it was like when we first met—when we were like that too?" At the time, we had been married for thirteen years!

When I think about the things I love most about our relationship, few thoughts rise more quickly to the surface than the fact that, after many years together, we are still very playful. Seldom do we take ourselves or each other too seriously. For the most part, the only times we're frustrated at one another is when we do.

When I think of all the couples I have known over the years, a vast majority of the happy ones are, to one degree or another, playful. They can be serious in other ways, but in their relationship together, they have the capacity to be silly—not overdone or all the time, but they have some degree of lightheartedness. They spend plenty of time laughing together, and at themselves. They don't take each other's habits, quirks, or imperfections very seriously. And when they do, it doesn't last very long. This light-hearted attitude keeps them from acting defensive, combative, or argumentative, and it keeps their expectations of one another in check and reasonable. It also helps them to keep their perspective, act as a team, and remain good friends. We've found that when you're playful and have a sense of humor, it's almost impossible to sweat the small stuff!

On the other hand, when I think of the couples I've known who seem troubled or not very happy together, they invariably seem too serious. For the most part, they are unable to laugh together. By no means do they allow themselves to be silly or playful. Life, including their relationship, is "serious business." This seems to translate into defensive communication, bickering, annoyance, and power struggles. When you're too serious, everything seems like a pretty big deal and it's easy to sweat the small stuff.

The best way to become more playful is to take yourself less seriously. Lighten up. Allow yourself to have some fun and stop caring so much what other people think about you—or what you might look like in the eyes of others.

Many people make the mistake of telling themselves they will be playful "later," when all their business is taken care of and when all their problems are solved—but for now, they must be serious. The problem is, our "business" will never be completely taken care of, we will always have problems, and there's always something we must attend to. So, don't wait until it's too late—life is short; be playful now.

44.

STOP REHEARSING

UNHAPPINESS

♥ Implementing this strategy can be a little tricky, but once you get the hang of it, it has the power to improve and even transform your relationships. The benefits you enjoy can be powerful and may occur almost immediately.

Here's an example of how it works: Kelly is driving to see her boyfriend. A memory comes to mind of an argument they had a few weeks ago. As she remembers the incident, she "plays it out again," almost as if it were happening right there in the car. She realizes that her boyfriend was being unnecessarily stubborn, maybe even a little mean. She remembers his doing something similar at a party last month. Doubt begins to creep into her mind. She begins to wonder if he's the right guy after all. Within a matter of minutes she's a little angry, as she thinks to herself, "He'd better not do that again tonight." By the time she arrives at his apartment, she's feeling slightly distant; nothing horrible, but enough to make a difference in the way she feels about the evening and about her relationship.

We refer to this type of inner dialogue as a "thought attack" because, in a sense, that's what it really is—your own thoughts attacking you. We say it's tricky because, for the most part, you're not even aware that you're doing it. Thoughts like these happen so quickly, and so often, that most of us don't even realize what's happening. And that's the real problem! We get lost in our thoughts in much the same way that we might get lost in a movie or in a good book. At times, like Kelly, most of us mistake a few harmless negative thoughts for a serious problem in our relationship. Consequently, rather than dismissing the thoughts and responding to each moment as it arrives, we instead take out our self-created frustration on our partner as if he or she were the real problem. And while it's possible there is a real problem, our minds have a way of blowing things out of proportion.

A thought attack can be about practically anything and can happen anywhere, at any time—in the shower, while you're trying to sleep, in an airplane, while walking the dog, as you're cleaning the house, at work, and elsewhere. Specifically, thought attacks can be about what's wrong in your relationship, how your needs aren't being met, or a fear or suspicion that's on your mind. People have reported to us having thought attacks about the fact that their partner isn't doing his or her fair share. Others play out worst-case scenarios about pending arguments, the implications of a diminishing sex drive, resentment over a partner's lack of ability to make an adequate income, or whatever.

We're certainly not suggesting that thinking about your relationship—your concerns, dreams, issues, or plans—is in any way wrong. In fact, doing so is often important, helpful, and nourishing. There is an enormous difference, however, between intentionally thinking about something—knowing what you're doing—versus being caught up in your thinking, engaged in a painful thought attack, and not even aware of what's going on.

The solution is simple, but not easy. All you have to do is catch yourself engaging in these tricky thought attacks. The idea is to see it happening, while it's happening. You observe yourself as the thinker. Once you see it, the rest is easy. You simply drop the thoughts, dismiss them, and let them go. You might say something like, "Oh, brother, there I go again," or something like that, some type of simple acknowledgment that you know what you're doing to yourself. Over time, it becomes much easier and you'll catch yourself much more quickly. Rather than engaging in a ten-minute inner conversation, you'll begin to observe it happening seconds after you start. Then, you can decide to think about the issue, or to simply let it go. Rather than being trapped, you'll have a choice.

Many people have shared with us that this has been the single most helpful insight they have ever had about themselves—the idea that they actually practice being unhappy, or harming their relationship, without even knowing it by mentally "rehearsing unhappiness." Without the ongoing distraction of negative mental rehearsal, what's usually left is the love and respect you have for your partner.

Once you begin to nip this problem in the bud, you'll notice a great deal more peace and happiness showing up in your relationship. Rather than giving significance to your negative thoughts, you can spend that energy thinking about more positive aspects of your relationship. We hope you'll give this strategy a fair try—it's fun and extremely effective, and it might just change your life.

45.

DON'T BE THE HERO OF
EVERY STORY

Most of us love to tell stories. We like to talk about something that happened to us—something we felt, observed, hoped for, or succeeded in achieving. It can even be satisfying to share our failures, mess-ups, and mishaps. Sharing is one of the most obvious ways two people become (or remain) close and intimate. It's also a way that we stay connected to and interested in one another.

Yet, there's a communication habit to become aware of, so insidious that it seems to creep into most relationships, at least some of the time. This habit is the need to be the hero of every story.

I was sitting in a restaurant in New York City waiting for a friend who was running late. At the table next to me was a young couple, probably in their mid to late twenties, apparently out on a date.

On three separate occasions, the young woman attempted to tell a story about something she had been through. The first story centered around someone who had been rude to her earlier that day. Next, she was sharing her frustration about how stressful and demanding her job had become. Finally, she told him a tear-jerking story about how her parents hadn't listened to her while she was growing up.

The first story ended with the young man insisting that his taxi driver, earlier that day, must have been even more rude than whoever it was that had been rude to her. After all, he said, "He was the worst I've ever seen." The second story ended even more abruptly when he described his own job as being one of the most stressful jobs imaginable. The last story ended with his own emotional description of his parents who had, in his words, "abused him emotionally."

As I glanced in the woman's eyes, I could sense an almost lifeless quality in her. The disappointment was obvious. Every time she had tried to share something of herself, it was followed up with a more significant story that had something to do with him. Nothing she said was quite good enough. I could imagine her disappointment, perhaps even pain, that yet another man had proven that he wasn't willing to simply listen and to allow her to be the hero of her own stories.

This is a difficult strategy to articulate because it's often very subtle. I'm quite sure this man had meant no harm whatsoever. In fact, my guess is that, from his perspective, he was merely engaging in a conversation, sharing back and forth. Unfortunately, he didn't see that he was stealing his date's thunder. As unintentional as it may have been, he was telling her, by his responses, that she wasn't quite important enough, or interesting enough. She needed his embellishment to make her stories come to life. Never once did he say (or even imply), "Hey, great story," or "Wow, that sounds like it must have been tough."

We've certainly done this to each other on many occasions and, hopefully, have learned from our mistakes. Our suggestion is this: Whenever possible, try to avoid editing, correcting, or even adding to your partner's story. Most importantly, don't bring the story back to yourself by saying something like, "That's nothing, listen to this." When you do, you are minimizing the story, making the silent statement that the story wasn't good enough, significant enough, or important enough to stand on its own. It needed your input to make it complete. Even though you may not have intended the slightest harm, it nevertheless sends a message that you're more interested in your part of the story than you are in listening to and fully appreciating your partner's tale.

If you can implement this strategy, at least most of the time, you'll probably observe a shift in your partner's enthusiasm and lightheartedness. He or she will, once again, delight in sharing with you. And because you are listening so intently, chances are your partner will want to listen to you as well. You'll both end up having more fun and enjoying each other like never before.

46.

MAKE THE FRESH-START
COMMITMENT

♥ It doesn't matter whether you've just met or fallen in love—or whether you've been together for many years—it can be enormously helpful to make the "fresh-start commitment." Doing so is the relationship version of "cleaning the slate" and making today, instead of yesterday or tomorrow, the most important day of your life together.

Making the fresh-start commitment means making the decision to drop all concerns, regrets, and disappointments from your past, as well as all of your expectations regarding the future. Today becomes the focal point of your relationship. This day becomes more important than past mistakes or future plans. You stop comparing today to days gone by—or your hopes of a better tomorrow. You ask yourself the question, "How can I make today the best day that it can possibly be?" The answer to this simple question becomes the key to a heartfelt and loving connection.

It's been said that "yesterday is but a dream, tomorrow a fantasy." Today, however, is reality—the only day that is guaranteed to be yours. The good news is that you have the capacity to make the precious moments of today all that they can be. You do so by dismissing your thoughts from the past and postponing your reactions of tomorrow—until they, too, become today. The trick is to forgive your past, become less fearful of the future, and bless the gift of today.

It's easy to see why this is a wise decision that can put your relationship on solid ground, or give it new life. If, for example, you've just met, it can be tempting to expect (or hope) that each time you get together is going to be like the last time, or that the magic you feel is somehow supposed to remain.

Avoiding this tendency is very difficult. It's human nature to want the good or exciting times to stay the same, to hang onto what feels good. If your partner is very attentive, for example, seemingly interested in everything you say, almost as though you're the only person in the world, it feels wonderful. Who wouldn't like to be treated like that? Yet, one of the laws of nature (and of relationships) is change—the fact that nothing (good or bad) stays the same. This doesn't mean your love and respect for one another won't become deeper, richer, or even more satisfying. It simply means that today's experience will never be exactly like yesterday's. If you resist this reality, you'll inevitably end up disappointed, longing for experiences of the past, demanding that your partner be the same. If you embrace it, however, you'll be free to enjoy one another each and every day.

If you've been together for a long time and are experiencing some trouble, the same principle applies in a slightly different way. If you expect the present moments of your relationship to be the same as they have been (difficult in some way), your expectation will keep your dissatisfaction alive. Your relationship will be stuck in the past. If, on the other hand, you can let go of the past, free yourself from it—your resentments, judgments, concerns, anger, boredom, and frustration—you'll open the door to a brand-new beginning. You will be making the fresh-start commitment.

The nice thing about this strategy is that it's easy and it really works. The present moments of your life are special and powerful. By immersing yourself in them, you give yourself the capacity to make every day the best day of your life.

47.

AVOID CORRECTING
EACH OTHER

We were in the lobby of a health club when a woman said to her husband, "See you later, honey. I've got to get home because I'd like to make you and the kids that casserole dish you love so much. It takes more than an hour and I want to have plenty of time." When I heard her say this, I thought to myself, "How thoughtful." My heart sank, however, when I heard her husband's response. Without even thinking about it, he fired back, "No it doesn't—it only takes about fifty minutes." Ouch.

A week or so later I was in a restaurant when I overheard a man telling a story to his wife and another couple at the table next to us. Obviously I wasn't paying much attention to the details, but he was talking for quite some time. All I heard was the last sentence, which he said with a satisfied chuckle. His punch line was, "We were just getting ready to leave when about ten people cut in front of us." It seemed like a good ending to a story and I found myself wishing I'd heard the whole thing. But before their friends had a chance to finish laughing, his wife blurted out, "There weren't ten people, John, there were only six."

Obviously these are somewhat obnoxious examples of the tendency many of us have to correct one another, particularly those we are closest to. Yet, we felt they were appropriate because they demonstrate how disrespectful and potentially damaging this habit can be to the quality of a relationship.

In both of these examples, and so many others, the "correction" was absolutely unnecessary. Other than being ignorant to the hurtful effects the correction has on the recipient, and the way it takes the joy out of sharing, the only possible motivation could be an attempt to be outright mean.

The woman in the health club was reaching out to her family. She was taking her valuable time and using it to express her love through her cooking. She was filled with enthusiasm as she proudly shared her plan with her husband. In return, he shot her down! There's no way to tell why he said what he did. My guess is he meant no harm and didn't even know he said it. But think about how it must have felt to her. What possible good did his comment make? Even if he was technically correct regarding the cooking time of the casserole, so what? How can being "right" be so much more important than protecting the feelings of someone you love? Rather than feeling appreciated, she probably felt minimized and deflated.

The same holds true with the wife who corrected her husband in front of their friends in the restaurant. Again, if you asked her, I doubt very much she would admit to ruining his story and his enjoyment and making him look a little foolish, on purpose. Instead, it was an innocent jab that took place because she hadn't taken the time to reflect on the destructive nature of correcting someone. Who cares how many people actually cut him off? What difference does it make?

Obviously, an isolated correction isn't going to make or break an otherwise nurturing relationship. We've all done it more than once. And keep in mind that if your partner corrects you every once in a while, you don't want to think of it as an emergency! It's not. Remember, the goal is to stop sweating the small stuff. However, you have to wonder why a person would continue to share stories, dreams, plans, and adventures with someone who was in the habit of correcting them. After a while, if someone you loved kept up the corrections, you'd become cautious and guarded, perhaps even distant.

The lesson here is simple. No one appreciates being corrected. In fact, most people resent it. So, unless there's a really good reason or you're dealing with an extremely important issue, it's a good rule of thumb to keep your corrections to yourself. Your partner will be able to share with you freely and openly, which will help keep your relationship fresh and alive.

48.

SIT IN SILENCE

Without question, one of the simplest, most peaceful, and, we believe, most leveraged ways to maintain a loving connection is to practice the art of sitting together, in silence. This beautiful yet seldom used practice brings forth compassion for one another while simultaneously strengthening the bond between you.

Think about the millions of words the average couple must share with one another over the course of their relationship: talking, arguing, negotiating, planning, remembering, bickering, and so forth. Few couples, regardless of how many years they spend together, will set aside any time whatsoever to simply sit quietly together, without saying a word. Yet, this silent communication may be one of the most important things you can do together as a couple. It can also be one of the most powerful and effective ways to communicate.

The practice itself is remarkably simple. You simply sit next to one another in a quiet, comfortable location. You can hold hands if you wish, but that's entirely up to you. You then close your eyes and clear your minds as well as you can. Breathe together, slowly and peacefully. Just sit, quietly and lovingly. You can do this together for a few minutes or longer, if you so desire.

Something magical happens when two people who share a connection sit together in silence. Defenses tend to drop and hearts open wide. By the time you open your eyes, you'll feel more peaceful and loving—to one another as well as to yourselves. Any friction you may have between you will have dissolved, or will at least be headed in that direction. It will be easier to see the innocence in each other and to love your partner for who he or she is, rather than insisting that they change in order to meet your expectations. You'll discover that any irritation you may have been feeling—or any tendency you were having to sweat the small stuff—will be fading away. You'll feel wiser and more compassionate and will probably feel like smiling.

Sitting together in silence has become one of the cornerstones of our relationship. We don't do it every day, nor do we make a big deal out of it, or talk about it very much. We just do it as often as it occurs to us—because it feels nice and keeps us connected at the heart. We usually sit together first thing in the morning while we're drinking our coffee.

Many of us have been taught that "communication" is critical in order to secure a good relationship—and this may be true. It's ironic, however, that one of the best and most loving ways to communicate is to do so without saying a word. So enjoy the silence, as well as the peace and warm feelings that come with it.

49.

TAKE RESPONSIBILITY FOR
YOUR OWN HAPPINESS

Unfortunately, one of the biggest relationship mistakes also happens to be one of the most tempting things to do if you are in a relationship: Make your partner responsible for your happiness and blame her when you are not!

It's a little scary to listen to many of the most popular songs on the radio. So often the message is, "You make me happy; I'd be lost without you; you are my world," or other, similar types of messages that take away all the power and responsibility to make yourself happy and put it on someone else. Wow! If you think about it, that's an enormous amount of pressure to put on another person. It's like saying, "I can't always be happy myself—but if you're going to be with me, you'd better make me happy."

On the surface, this concept seems rather obvious, but how many of us really do take full responsibility for our own happiness? How often do we say to ourselves, "Why can't my wife be different?" or "It makes me so mad when my husband acts that way," or "I'm stressed because my husband works too many hours." When you examine these (and thousands of other) very common statements and thoughts, it becomes clear that they suggest, however subtly, that somehow, someone other than you is responsible for your happiness. The thinking is like this: "If only he (or she) were different, I'd be happy. They have to change. Not me, no way. It's them!"

What we've found is that if you believe that the answer to your unhappiness lies in someone else's hands (no matter how much you love them), you're in for a load of trouble. Even if they manage to accommodate you with occasional changes, you'll come to rely on those changes for your continued happiness. There will be only one possible result. Eventually, you'll be let down and will be discouraged. You'll be left with that helpless and dependent "It's her fault" feeling.

Don't get us wrong. We're not saying your partner doesn't play a role in your happiness, or that you're not the happiest when you are together—or that you wouldn't or shouldn't be devastated if your partner left you by choice, or by circumstance. We certainly feel that way about each other—as do all of the happy couples we know. We're also not suggesting that there are not dramatic examples where it's clear that one partner is imposing on the other's chances of being happy.

What we are saying is that, ultimately, you and you alone are responsible for making yourself happy. When your life isn't working, you need to make changes or see things differently. You may have to make difficult choices, have painful or uncomfortable discussions, or compromise in some way—but you have to take responsibility for your own level of happiness. There isn't a relationship good enough to do it for you.

This is a very empowering insight for both you and your partner. In effect, you are making a statement to yourself that, while your relationship is absolutely a top priority and your love of your partner is immense, you have the power and the ability to make yourself happy. This means that you are okay when things aren't going so well or when your partner proves to be human. Your happiness isn't entirely dependent on your partner's acting in a very specific, predetermined way.

You are also making an important statement to your partner, taking a great deal of pressure off that person: "It's okay for you to be human. You can make mistakes and you don't have to walk around on eggshells or pretend to be a certain way when you're near me. You don't have to worry that I'll freak out every time you disappoint me. I accept the fact that when I'm disappointed, the disappointment is coming from my own thoughts. I have preferences, but won't allow those preferences to ruin my life. You can have low moods and you even have my permission to be less than perfect. I'm okay even when you're not okay, and I love you as unconditionally as I know how."

By taking responsibility for your own happiness, you open the door to a new type of relationship, one based on honesty, responsibility, courage, and wisdom. If you take this road, you're in for a lifetime of nice surprises. You'll be amazed at how much happier you'll be when you put the responsibility for your own happiness where it belongs—with you.

50.

MASTER THE ART OF THE
HEART-TO-HEART

♥ Regardless of how good, honest, loving, and wonderful your relationship happens to be—or becomes—it's inevitable that you are going to run into at least some degree of conflict. Every couple has occasional issues to resolve. It's built into the system. That's why it's essential that you master the art of this type of communication. I can't imagine a relationship surviving—certainly not thriving—without the use of this powerful tool.

A heart-to-heart is a very specific type of conversation that is ideally suited to—you guessed it—matters of the heart. You can use heart-to-heart talks to discuss awkward, painful, or difficult issues, or as a way to resolve conflict, solve problems, or come to a mutual understanding. In many instances, you can even use them as a way to agree to disagree. This is a loving yet extremely powerful way to communicate with someone you love. It's so powerful, in fact, that almost nothing is too painful to discuss, given the proper environment.

The foundation of a heart-to-heart talk is an agreement by each person to approach the conversation with love and respect. Both parties agree to speak and, even more importantly, listen, in a nondefensive manner, to keep their hearts open and their reactions in check. The overriding goals of a heart-to-heart talk are to ensure that each partner feels heard—and to ensure that both people emerge feeling closer to one another, regardless of whether or not the issue is ultimately resolved. The key is to bring up the need for a heart-to-heart in a gentle, nonthreatening manner and then to continue with the same attitude throughout your discussion. In a heart-to-heart, it's far more important to learn than it is to teach—to listen rather than speak. It's important to let go of your foregone conclusions and habitual reactions. It's important to absorb what is being said—rather than react to it.

So often, couples fall into poor communication habits with one another, with everyday stuff as well as with more sensitive issues. Most couples have plenty of knee-jerk reactions: blaming, jealousy, poor listening, taking for granted, and angry responses to contend with. These habits invariably lead to a lack of trust, an apathetic attitude, a distancing, or even outright disrespect or outrage.

Cultivating the respect for, and the desire to engage in, heart-to-heart talks can erase most, if not all, of these problems. And luckily, this type of communication is easy to implement. In most cases, it only takes one partner to positively influence the relationship by initiating this heartfelt communication. There are vastly different degrees of depth to a heart-to-heart talk—but any steps in this direction can be enormously helpful.

Shared intimacy or deep, honest communication is a profound need of the human spirit. Very simply, it's nourishing and brings with it a feeling of closeness. Sadly, if for whatever reasons you can't or aren't willing to share or listen at this level, your partner may drift away from you, emotionally or even physically. Over time, many people are far more comfortable sharing with other friends, even strangers, than they are with their spouse or significant other. In extreme cases, a partner will leave in search of someone who will listen, someone who is capable of communicating from the heart.

There's no formal structure to a heart-to-heart, nor is there a right or wrong way to do it. Essentially, all you have to do is agree that it's time for a heartfelt talk. You need to check in with one another to be sure the timing is right. If either of you is feeling defensive or stubborn, it's not the right time. Or, if you are attached to your "agenda," it's better to wait until later. But if the two of you are in a loving, receptive mood and feel you can discuss the issue in an unheated, nonreactive way, then it's a good time to go to it. Once you start, pause often. Reflect honestly on how well you are doing. You can even ask each other questions like, "Is this okay?" Or feel free to check in with your partner with statements like, "What I'm hearing you say is . . . am I hearing you correctly?" Be sure you're not being overbearing, defensive, reactive, or too aggressive. If you are, that's okay too. Gently back off and try again. Be patient and, above all, loving.

Over the years, Kris and I have had hundreds of heart-to-heart talks— some very light, concerning day-to-day annoyances (when we're sweating the small stuff), and others far more serious. We've discussed everything from disorganized closets and lost household items, to finances and career issues, to issues with the kids, to problems between the two of us. In every single instance, the heart-to-heart talk has played a major role in getting us through the problem. We hope you'll explore and experiment with this magical communication tool—it has worked wonders for us and, we believe, will do so for you as well.

51.

DON'T CONFUSE YOUR OWN
FRUSTRATION WITH A PROBLEM
IN THE RELATIONSHIP

I suppose it's human nature (at least a common human impulse), when you're frustrated, to try to figure out why you're feeling so bad, to pinpoint blame, or to come up with some logical rationale to explain your predicament. So when you're down in the dumps or in some way frustrated, you may think, "If I only knew why I was so upset, I'd start to feel better."

Then it hits you! "That's it—I know what it is—my relationship has some problems!" Immediately, you get into your detective mode and start to think of all the ways your relationship isn't what it should be. You mentally review your partner's imperfections and the ways your needs aren't being met. You analyze the ways your relationship isn't working right, the ways it isn't what it used to be, and the areas that need some work. Sometimes this tendency is minor; other times it's severe. Either way you've opened the door for, at the very least, some additional frustration, if not some actual trouble.

If you step back from this tendency, however, you'll begin to see that, most of the time, it's precisely because you are frustrated that problems and issues in your relationship are coming to mind. In other words, the frustration came first, and out of that frustration came the tendency to see, create, and analyze problems. When you're feeling agitated, stressed, irritated, bothered, or tired, or when you're in a negative state of mind, it's absolutely predictable that you're going to fill your head with negative thinking and your relationship will often be seen as the cause of your negative feelings. So, virtually any explanation you come up with—or that someone suggests to you when you're feeling bad—is going to seem to make logical sense to you while you're feeling down. You'll think to yourself something like, "My wife isn't supportive enough," or "My boyfriend isn't a good listener," and because you're feeling down, it will almost always seem to make perfect sense. You'll be able to validate your feelings with plenty of specific examples. Sadly, when you're feeling down or insecure, almost anything can seem problematic—you'll probably be sweating everything! And what's more, it will all seem to make perfect sense. This is one of those mental traps that doesn't get easier over time. Whether your relationship is brand new or you've been married fifty years, the same dynamic applies.

This isn't to say that the problems you notice and think about when you're feeling bad are never true—sometimes they are. However, if you think you have a problem when you're feeling bad and that problem is legitimate, it will certainly still seem that way when your mood is much higher and you're feeling good again. Not always, but a vast majority of the time, the problems that look so real and significant when you're feeling low magically disappear when you're in a better frame of mind. It happens much of the time.

The implication of this strategy is very simple and can change the course of your relationships forever. When you're feeling down, don't take your thoughts and feelings as seriously. When you're feeling down, you have less wisdom, compassion, perspective, and common sense. Instead of saying, "I know why I'm down—it's her or him, or the relationship," say to yourself, "Of course I'm feeling angry or frustrated; I'm in a low mood. I'm not in the right frame of mind to see things clearly." Instead of reacting, wait it out. Pay less attention to your thinking, give it less significance, and, above all, avoid analyzing. If you do, you'll immunize and protect yourself and your relationship from a vast majority of day-to-day issues. The less attention you pay to your negative thoughts and feelings, the quicker your mood will rise and your wisdom will return.

Of course, this is easier said than done. While this advice is very simple, it isn't always easy. The reason is, each time you're frustrated, you'll probably be compelled to revert to the human tendency of trying to make sense of it all. Yet, if you're patient and if you practice a bit, you'll get the hang of it. And when you do, it will be worth the effort.

52.

STOP BEING SO DEFENSIVE

If you could eliminate all defensiveness in your personality, you would not only have the best relationship in town but, in fact, you would become the most loving and adorable person on this planet. You'd have so much charisma and charm, you'd be almost irresistible, a virtual magnet for human companionship. People would flock to be in your presence, and you and your partner would live happily ever after.

Let's be realistic. No one can eliminate all of their defensive reactions; it's part of being human. Everyone seems to get defensive at least some of the time because no one likes to be criticized, questioned, attacked, judged, lectured, or spoken down to. However, with some gentle effort, we've found that it's relatively easy to make great strides in the direction of becoming less defensive.

As the word suggests, being "defensive" means that we are feeling the need to defend ourselves. Emotionally, we coil up, tighten, and resist the comments (sometimes even the thoughts) that are being directed toward us. We do these things in an attempt to protect ourselves, as part of our built-in "fight or flight" response.

It's both fortunate and unfortunate that our knee-jerk defensive responses never seem to keep us from feeling hurt, rejected, or insecure. It's unfortunate because, if they worked, we'd all be feeling pretty secure. We would have a strategy that could keep us from feeling dejected whenever we felt criticized. But if you pay close attention to how you actually feel after any type of defensive response, you'll notice that you end up feeling even worse. It seems to do nothing more than put salt in the wound.

The good news, however—the "fortunate" side of the failure of defensiveness—is that, because it works so poorly, it tells us there must be a better way. And there is.

The alternative to feeling or acting defensive is called acceptance. Unlike defensiveness, which is like tightening your fist and becoming stubborn, acceptance is like releasing your fist and becoming open and receptive. When you strive for acceptance, you are attempting to receive life—including criticism, comments you disagree with, and all the rest—with a degree of equanimity.

Acceptance is not about becoming a doormat, nor is it about becoming apathetic. Neither is it about changing your most treasured beliefs. Instead, acceptance is about becoming slightly more open and receptive to what others have to say. It's about becoming less reactive and a better listener.

At first, because it may feel foreign, a more accepting attitude and response to life may be a little difficult. To get started requires a leap of faith—the willingness to try a softer approach. This is one of those beautiful experiences, however, that gets much easier with each attempt. Once you see how much easier your life and your relationships become, you'll be hooked—you'll lose your desire to fight back so much.

Once you're on your way, you'll find yourself choosing your battles more wisely. When something is truly important or worth defending, you'll certainly make the effort—but with "small stuff," you'll be more inclined to stay a little more detached. When someone lashes out at you—or criticizes you—you'll remain calm and be able to decide whether or not there is any validity in the comments. You'll either learn from the experience or you'll wisely let it go. Either way, it won't affect you nearly as much as it used to.

There are enormous dividends that come with becoming less defensive. Your partner will respond to your change of heart by being easier to be around—and will probably become less defensive too. In addition, your learning curve will become sharper. Instead of reacting to criticism or suggestions with anger, fear, and withdrawal, you'll find yourself interested in the other point of view. You'll have more heart-to-heart conversations and far fewer adversarial conflicts.

Why not give it a try? What have you got to lose, other than a habitual response that interferes with your relationship's being all that it can be?

53.

BE CONSISTENTLY
GRATEFUL

Nothing keeps a relationship fresh, alive, and nourishing than genuine feelings of gratitude. And, on the flip side, nothing dooms a relationship to failure more than a lack of it. Indeed, gratitude is one of the primary ingredients of a mutually nurturing relationship.

Gratitude is important for many reasons. It keeps your heart open and your mind receptive to the gifts of life and of your relationship. It serves as a constant reminder of how fortunate you are to be alive, and keeps you from taking your relationship for granted. Gratitude keeps you feeling satisfied, reminding you that what you have is good enough. When you are focused on gratitude, it keeps your problems in perspective, especially the small ones. It immunizes you from being bothered by your partner's little quirks and the imperfections in your relationship. Gratitude allows you to see beyond the "small stuff" and keeps you from overreacting to the hassles and issues of being in a relationship.

Beyond your own satisfaction, however, the expression of gratitude keeps your bond secure and loving. Everyone loves to know (and hear) that they are appreciated and valued. In fact, when someone feels taken for granted, or underappreciated, resentment or apathy is usually not too far away. A lack of gratitude is a major factor in a relationship becoming stagnant and boring. Couples stop caring so much because they don't feel acknowledged and appreciated. Often, people start asking the question, "What difference does it make?"

By being consistently grateful and by expressing your feelings of gratitude, you are reinforcing the fact that your relationship is a gift—which it is. Gratitude is a powerful force that can eliminate and overcome most problems that exist in a relationship. In other words, you can do a lot of things wrong, make mistakes, and prove to be very human—as long as you remember to be grateful.

It's easy to get into the habit of taking one another for granted. The combination of the passing of time, familiarity with one another, and the hustle and bustle of life seems to take over and consume us. Somewhere along the line, we forget how special and valuable our loved one is to us and how much they bring to our life. However, with some gentle attention, it's also easy to develop an "attitude of gratitude." You start by taking your focus off of what's wrong and what's not working, and replacing that focus with a sincere commitment to reflect on all that's right in your life—and in your relationship. That's it! The rest will take care of itself. As you think about what's right, you'll begin noticing and appreciating the contribution and love that your partner brings to your life. Then, as you begin to express your appreciation for what you are noticing, your relationship will be fed the nourishment it needs to deepen and thrive.

I received a beautiful letter from a reader that sums up the power of gratitude. To paraphrase, it reads: "I used to think . . . now I realize." It all gets down to how you look at it. In the end, you'll see what you're looking for. If your mind is on the lookout for what's right and beautiful in your relationships, that is what you'll see—and that will be the essence of your relationship.

147

54.

DON'T FALL INTO THE "I'VE GOT TIME FOR EVERYONE BUT YOU" TRAP

We've seen this easy-to-fall-into trap hurt so many couples that it's almost painful to write about. As most of us know all too well, it's easy to get overwhelmed with all the responsibilities of life, to fall short of time and find ourselves scrambling, in desperate need of cutting back our schedule. As the saying goes, "Something has to give."

Unfortunately, without even knowing it and with no harmful intent whatsoever, it's often our loved ones who get pushed to the back of the line. In other words, in our efforts to get everything done, we end up neglecting the people we love most in the world—our partner, children, or others we love deeply. Sadly, when we do, we put a hurtful wedge between ourselves and those we love. No one wants to feel as though everything and everyone is more important than they are. It hurts when there seems to be time for everyone and everything—except you.

We find time for work—plenty of it. And, of course, it's so easy to justify this one—after all, almost everyone "has to work." Then there are the ongoing chores—too many to even mention here. There may be home projects that must, at some point, get done. Then there's our community or church involvement—how could we ever cut these out? Who would want to? There are all those social obligations, as well, one right after the other. We want to be a good friend, neighbor, person—how could we let these go? Finally, we may have interests of our own, a need for exercise, a hobby perhaps. The list goes on and on.

If we're not careful, slowly but surely we begin neglecting the special people in our lives, spending less time and feeling more distracted. It's not intentional. It just happens. You may start coming home late more often, or travel more frequently. Dates get canceled or shortened. Your special times become less and less frequent—or you begin to combine them with other activities. When you're home you're usually doing something else, probably something "productive"—cleaning, yard work, fixing something. Or you're involved in the kids' school—or doing your taxes, or whatever.

Obviously, we *do* have tremendously busy lives and many important and time-consuming responsibilities. It's certainly the case that sacrifices and compromises will have to be made by all of us. We only have so many hours in the day, and none of us can do everything. We're certainly not suggesting you drastically change the way you spend your time or completely rearrange your priorities to spend a great deal of additional time together.

On the other hand, it's important to become aware of this tendency—and to see how easily it can sneak into your relationship. It's helpful to reflect on the messages you're *really* sending to your partner. Even though you may love your partner more than anything in the world, the messages you are sending may contradict this love. The old cliché, "Your actions speak louder than your words," is really true.

There may be no perfect way to completely overcome this tendency—we sure haven't found one. However, it's enormously helpful (on a regular basis) to honestly reflect on your relationship and see where this habit may already be sneaking into place or where it's likely to in the future. Doing so can assist you in making any necessary adjustments, learning to say no to other requests, setting boundaries and limits, or breaking habits that are interfering with your loving connection. We hope, as we have, that you find this useful.

55.

ORGANIZE A CHARITABLE
PROJECT TOGETHER

Virtually no activity has the potential of bringing two people closer together than carrying out a project for a good cause or, more specifically, organizing and executing a charitable project all on your own. This is a strategy worth serious consideration because, while many couples are extremely kind and generous people, and might even regularly participate in good causes through private giving, projects through their church, volunteering, or in some other way, a very small percentage of couples will set out to jointly put together a project all on their own, and experience the joyful effects of pure giving. The rewards to your relationship are significant and lasting. You will develop camaraderie, increased gratitude for the gifts you already share, and a deeper perspective, which will help you let go of minor irritations that usually seem more significant than they really are.

In the flurry of everyday life, it's easy to get caught up in our own worlds—to become frustrated by the demands of life. And while there's no question that life can be frustrating, even overwhelming at times, it's equally true that doing something for others or for a cause we believe in helps to reduce that frustration. By putting some of our attention on "doing good," and a little of our effort and time into something other than our own "stuff," we remind ourselves that there's more to life than meets the eye—that our problems, especially the small ones, can usually be put into perspective. But more than that, we get to experience the pure joy of giving—of seeing something through, start to finish, that is purely positive and unselfish, something that has nothing to do with "us," or with our ordinary day-to-day existence.

Our first project together was a grassroots food drive we planned during our trip to India. The suffering we were witnessing reminded us how fortunate we were to have our basic needs met, including having food on the table. It also reminded us of how many people back home were in need of help. While we were already in the habit of donating money and food to reputable organizations, we had never planned our own event. Despite the fact that our project was extremely small by almost any standard, and completely unsophisticated in nature, planning it turned out to be a significant moment in our lives. It was then that we dedicated our lives to kindness and service. We saw how incredibly easy it was to do something for others and how much joy it brought to our lives and to our relationship. Mother Teresa once said, "We cannot do great things on this earth. We can only do small things with great love." This was a perfect example of her conviction. It was very small—but filled with love.

Essentially, all we did was this: We sent out a heartfelt letter to virtually everyone we knew within a certain radius, asking them to donate at least one large grocery bag of nonperishable food. Our premise was that a request from friends would be taken more seriously than a request from a stranger. We followed up every letter with a personal phone call and asked everyone to ask their neighbors to participate as well. We made it really easy for everyone so that it would be almost impossible for them not to participate. We picked a date and rented a big truck. We had everyone leave their contribution on their doorstep the morning of our designated day. We called everyone two days prior to remind them and asked them, once again, to see if their neighbors would participate by leaving their contribution on our friends' doorsteps.

The response was overwhelmingly positive, almost unbelievable. Not only did virtually everyone we asked participate, but many convinced their neighbors to do so as well. We would arrive at a home to not one or two, but sometimes ten or twelve, large bags of food. It was almost as if everyone did their own mini-food drive—and we simply picked it all up and delivered it. In addition, many people wrote us beautiful cards or notes, thanking us for our efforts and telling us what a great idea they thought it was. It took all day, but we filled the entire truck with food, stacked to the brim, and delivered it to an incredible church that passes out food to the homeless on a daily basis. They were extremely grateful and told us that it was one of the largest donations they had ever received from ordinary citizens. Knowing that the food would be consumed by people who really needed it was one of the most satisfying feelings either one of us had ever experienced. We realized that, had our efforts amounted to even a single bag of food, it would have been well worth the effort. It wasn't the amount of food—it was the love that was most important.

The next day we wrote a thank you letter to everyone who had participated and told them of the success of the project and how we had grown in the process. We can't measure what, if any, effect our project had on others, but our sense was that many people began to think of ways that they might also be a little more helpful to the community. It seems that, often, when a seed is planted, a positive chain of events soon follows. But whether our project had an effect on our friends, acquaintances, and neighbors was secondary. We know that the time we spent organizing our project had a positive effect on our relationship that has lasted to this day.

56.

ASK YOURSELF THE QUESTION, "IN THE SCHEME OF THINGS, IS THIS REALLY THAT BIG A DEAL?"

When you get right down to it, at the heart of learning not to sweat the small stuff is the art of beginning to recognize that many of the things that we treat as a really big deal . . . aren't. We blow things out of proportion, making them seem far more significant; we read into things, over-analyze, anticipate the worst, get uptight, rehearse unhappiness in our mind, and turn molehills into mountains. Once we turn the corner, however, and begin to put things into their proper perspective, we're on the road to a more peaceful life.

Simple as it sounds (and it is really simple), it can be enormously helpful to ask yourself the question, whenever you're feeling a little uptight, "In the scheme of things, is this really that big a deal?" In most cases, the simple act of asking the question is all that needs to be done. The question will gently but firmly jolt you into reality, and immediately you'll become more reflective and increase your level of perspective. You'll find yourself saying things to yourself like, "Oh well," and "Whatever."

Both Kris and I have learned to do this quite effectively, and it has, over and over again, helped us to let go of the small stuff and get on with our day. Whether it involves something like forgetting to do one of our chores, engaging in an irritating habit, or forgetting to do a favor we had promised to do, we're usually able to remind ourselves that it's not that big a deal, and let it go. I remember a day when Kris was going out the door to pick up a few things from the store. There was an article I wanted to see in the newspaper really badly, so I reminded her three times not to forget to buy a paper. She did forget.

Ten years ago, I suspect I would have given her a bad time, as I suspect many married couples would do, given the circumstance. I've learned, however, to laugh this and other things like it off as if they were insignificant—which, in the scheme of things, they most certainly are. I now see stuff like this as really "small stuff." And I've noticed that, as I have demanded less perfection and have increased my patience, Kris has responded by almost never forgetting. And when she proves again to be human, it's okay too.

Kris regularly gives me the same slack. Rather than freaking out and getting uptight when my plane is canceled or I'm overcommitted, or when I act less than loving, she reminds herself that, although it's disappointing and perhaps a temporary hassle, it's really not that big a deal. And, to be honest, there are times when each of us gets really upset and does revert to losing our perspective. But we've learned that that's no big deal either.

A friend once told me that she believes, "If someone is dying, seriously hurt, or in serious danger, it's a really big deal. Otherwise, it's really not." Neither Kris nor I feel we have mastered this strategy, but we know we're moving in the right direction. And you can too!

57.

DON'T CONTINUE DOING THE
SAME THINGS AND EXPECT
A DIFFERENT RESULT

Our family was visiting an aquarium when we observed a most curious thing. For about fifteen minutes we watched a beautiful sea turtle swim gracefully around a large tank. Each time the turtle would pass by a certain spot, he would bump his fin and part of his head into the glass, in exactly the same way. It was clear that he wasn't being hurt, but it did appear to an untrained eye as though each time he hit the glass, he was quite surprised.

I once heard someone describe the definition of insanity as "doing the same thing over and over but expecting a different result." And while I wouldn't pretend to know what the turtle was attempting to accomplish, and would therefore never call him insane, there does seem to be a certain logic to that definition when applied to us humans.

How often do we overreact, lash out in frustration, sweat the small stuff, or respond in a knee-jerk manner to someone we love (our partner or potential partner, child, friend, colleague, or parent), and receive, in return, a response we don't like? Then, the next time we're frustrated, we use the same response—and we get the same result. Over and over again, we repeat the same mistake. You'd think after thousands and thousands of attempts, we'd get the message. But usually we don't!

Mary was a bright young women. She had a wonderful sense of humor and was very attractive. She seemed to have everything going for her—health, looks, a great career, ambition, compassion, intelligence, and wit, among other things. When I met her, it seemed as though she had only one visible flaw. She was extremely jealous. She would get into a relationship and all would go well. Then, out of the blue, she would fly into a jealous rage over some really minor thing—her partner would mention an old girlfriend, or talk about a woman friend at work, or indicate his desire to go backpacking alone—or some other equally innocent part of his life. Over and over again, she would frighten her partners away by her reactions. She told me she had been involved in more than a dozen relationships in recent years and that every one of them had broken up under similar circumstances.

Admittedly, hers is an extreme example. Yet, like the rest of us, Mary's mistake was that she kept expecting (or hoping) for a different response. She told me that, deep down, she longed for a man who wouldn't make her jealous. She somehow felt that a dramatic reaction on her part would help her partner get into line. It never worked—but she kept trying. She didn't realize that the problem wasn't the men she was dating, but her own knee-jerk reactions to their words and behavior.

Happily, as she saw her own contribution to the problem, she was able to make some major adjustments in her responses. To a large degree, she was able to stop doing things the same way. And, at very least, when she reverted to her old behavior, she knew she wasn't going to get a different result. She was even able to develop a sense of humor about her silly reactions. Needless to say, her relationships improved. (And probably lasted longer, too!)

To one degree or another, we all share this problem. The two of us are certainly no exception. Whether it's our typical reaction to criticism or suggestions—or the way we fail to listen carefully and instead finish other people's sentences, or something totally different—there is usually some way that we do the same thing over and over yet expect a different response. By making an honest assessment of your own tendencies, you can nip this problem in the bud. In doing so, your relationships will improve and you'll save yourself a great deal of frustration.

58.

RESPOND WITH LOVE

There's no question that this will be one of the simplest and perhaps most obvious suggestions in this book. It remains, however, at the root of a loving relationship. It's not always easy, of course, but it's almost always the best course of action and the best attitude to embrace.

When you respond with love—not jealousy, anger, resentment, selfishness, or frustration, but simply love—you've all but guaranteed a loving interaction and, in the long run, a loving and successful partnership. Rather than sweating the small stuff, you'll be appreciating the big stuff! You'll be nondefensive, nonreactive, and accepting. You'll find that everything important in your relationship will magically fall into place, including the difficulties. The reason: Love heals. When you respond with love, your partner respects you, loves you, wants to be with you, and wants you to be happy. Compromise is easy, as is forgiveness. Responding with love helps you see the innocence in your partner, yourself, and all of humanity. When you respond with love, it's easy for your partner to see his or her flaws without feeling defensive or threatened. Likewise, when your partner responds with love, it's easy for you to see your contribution to any problems you may be having.

I've thought a great deal about this idea and I simply can't poke any holes in it. Every great spiritual teacher and respected spiritual tradition advocates this position—and every great spiritual book is filled with this wisdom. Further, when you talk to happy couples about their suggestions for a strong relationship, this is always, 100 percent of the time, at or near the top of their list.

It's been said and expressed in so many different ways, but the message is the same—simply put, "Respond with love, and all will be well." The most consistent objection to this suggestion is, "I already do—but my partner won't." If you feel this way, it's likely that you're not responding with enough love. Obviously there are rare exceptions such as when abuse is involved—but most of the time, all that is needed is more love.

Here are two mundane, day-to-day examples. Example one: Suppose your partner walks into the house in a sour mood and slams the door. What should you do? One response would be to yell out in an irritated tone, "What's wrong with you?" Or, might it be better to simply be patient, understanding, and loving? There's no prescription to describe exactly what you might say or do. Instead, your actions unfold naturally when your heart is responding with love.

Example two: What happens if your partner accuses you of something you know in your heart isn't true—you're not contributing enough or doing enough, for example? You can act, feel, and respond defensively, as most people probably would do. You could lash back with hurtful comments of your own. Of course, this would virtually guarantee ongoing negative feelings for both of you. On the other hand, what if you responded with love? What if, instead of reacting to the comments with anger or some other familiar reaction, you simply remained loving and kind? What if you said something like, "I'm sorry you feel that way," without the slightest sarcasm or hint of anger in your voice? What if you didn't demand that your partner was loving in order that you remained loving? What do you think would happen? Imagine, for a moment, how quickly most issues would dissolve and go away. Imagine how much more time would be spent loving, instead of being irritated at each other.

Obviously, no one is perfect and no one responds with love all the time—certainly not the two of us. But we can tell you honestly that this is our goal. And I'd say that although we have a long way to go, we respond with love far more often than ever before.

It seems to us that if responding with love is not a goal and a priority in your relationship, it's not going to happen. You may spend your entire life waiting for your partner to change and to become more loving—or you may end up waiting for that perfect partner: that person who will never act in ways that you don't approve of. Narrow odds! One thing we're certain of is this: Any couple can be happier, more loving, and less inclined to sweat the small stuff if they commit individually and collectively to respond with love.

59.

LOOK IN THE MIRROR

♥ So often, when we're angry or frustrated at the one we love, something else is secretly going on beneath the surface—we're angry or frustrated at ourselves. That's right, ourselves. But because it's easier to put the blame on someone else, and our partner is the person closest to us, we often blame them instead of looking in the mirror and facing the facts.

Shortly after we had our first child, Kris and I went through a brief period of time when I was unusually frustrated at what I thought was her. I expressed frustration that I was "doing too much." I was working full time, attending graduate school, and trying very hard to be a good husband and new father. When Kris would take time for herself, work out at the gym, or spend time with her friends, I would feel a twinge of resentment. I would ask myself questions like, "Why does she have time to herself when I'm always scrambling?" It didn't seem fair—I was always, 100 percent of the time, either working, studying, or spending time with our baby. And although I loved everything I was doing—especially being a dad—I had no time to myself. I was tired and burned out.

At some point, Kris sensed my frustration and asked that we have a heart-to-heart talk about it. As is usually the case when two people in love let down their defenses and open up, the obvious truth came out. The reality was this: I wasn't really mad at Kris. In fact, I envied her ability to work part time, spend enormous time and energy with our daughter—and yet, somehow, manage to squeeze a little time in for herself, at least once in a while. The truth was, she had her priorities straight and I was jealous. She was pacing herself, honoring her rhythm, and putting the odds in her favor that she could keep her sense of well-being. I, on the other hand, was doing everything possible to ensure a nervous breakdown!

Looking back, I can see that it was easier to blame Kris than it was to admit that I (and I alone) had allowed my life to get a little out of control. I had taken on too many commitments—some necessary, others somewhat optional. I was upset that there was no time left for me and that, unlike Kris, I didn't value myself enough to leave even a few minutes a day for me. But rather than take responsibility for my decisions, I acted a little like a martyr or victim.

Our discussion (and Kris's wisdom) helped me to see that life would surely go on if I allowed myself a little time. In fact, I learned that life would become both easier and more enjoyable, as it had been in the past, if I would learn to operate at a healthier pace.

The moment I realized that my frustration had nothing to do with Kris and instead had everything to do with me, everything changed. I felt more peaceful and in control. In addition, I felt reconnected to Kris and, in fact, had even more respect for her than ever before. Instead of judging her choices, I admired them. I tried to learn from her.

I discovered something that I have since accepted as an absolute truth: When you take care of yourself and are good to yourself, you have plenty of energy to attend to your responsibilities, lovingly and effectively.

It's so tempting to partially or even fully blame our partner for our frustrations in life. The idea of looking in the mirror applies to so many different aspects of human relations. Often when you're frustrated, this is a signal that something is going on with you. Our suggestion is this: The next time you feel angry, resentful, jealous, or frustrated by your partner, use it as an opportunity to look carefully in the mirror. What you discover may save your sanity—and your relationship.

60.

ALLOW YOUR PARTNER
TO BE HUMAN

At the heart of our friendship, love relationship, and marriage is our acceptance of and, in fact, our conscious embracing of the fact that we are two human beings doing the very best that we can. It's true that we love and respect each other—very much—and we are committed in every sense of the word, till death do us part. Yet, we both understand that, in reality, we're just two ordinary people. This mutual acceptance of our humanness keeps our relationship rich, loving, alive, nourishing, and interesting.

Sounds remarkably obvious, and it is. Yet, how many couples forget this oh-so-important fact of life? How many of us become angry, jealous, or resentful when our partner turns out to be none other than human? How many of us are more tolerant and patient with complete strangers than we are with our partner? How many of us put near-impossible expectations on our partner that could only be met by someone other than a fellow human? How often do we forget to make allowances in our heart for the fact that our partner is a human being?

Human beings are very complex. We are, as Zorba the Greek once said, "The whole catastrophe." We make mistakes. We change. At times, we say the wrong thing and disappoint others, including those we love. We often use good judgment, but at other times our judgment is not so good. Some of our decisions are wise; others are not. We have bad moods and bad days, and sometimes we get depressed. We become insecure and lose our way. We don't always listen well. Most of us sweat the small stuff—in love and elsewhere. We have doubts and fears. And all of us have at least a little bit of self-interest, fear, greed, and lust—if not in our actions, at least in our imaginations. You can pretend that you don't—you can deny it, you can hide it, perhaps even overcome it—but the truth is, you're human. Even when you're completely committed to your partner, you have other concerns and agendas going in your head, and in your life.

When you're in a love relationship, it's easy to forget who you're in the relationship with—a fellow human. You're not with a perfect person, someone who is incapable of letting you down, someone who has successfully risen above all confusion, or someone who is less human than everyone else.

We've known men who resent, even divorce, over things we wouldn't even think twice about—a partner who questions his judgment, talks to her friends about him, has legitimate passions apart from marriage and family, or who desires to spend time alone, away from her spouse on occasion. But that's what some women do—they're human. Why is that wrong? And we've known women who go crazy if their boyfriend or husband wants to watch a ballgame or looks at an attractive woman or has a female friend. But these are a few of the things that some guys do—they're human too.

I suppose the assumption for many people is that once we commit or get married, our partner is no longer allowed to be human. So we make up rules, and when they are broken we go crazy or feel hurt, jealous, or angry. We sabotage our relationship—simply because our partner is human. It's little wonder so many relationships are lifeless or completely void of honest communication. Who would want to be honest or share with someone who didn't allow them to be human? Not us.

There are many problems associated with not allowing your partner to be human. We've already mentioned the obvious—it's unrealistic. But more than that, when you don't allow your partner to be human, you put a wall between each other. If your partner can't share his or her dreams with you without criticism, they will stop sharing—guaranteed. If you can't discuss your fears without being lectured, you'll turn to others who will listen. Indeed, most couples lose their friendships as well as their intimacy, largely because they stop allowing one another to be human. Chances are, they'll push their partner away—either figuratively or literally.

We're not talking about putting up with affairs or other destructive behavior. Yet, there is something remarkably freeing and magical about seeing each other as human beings instead of demanding something that isn't realistic or, we believe, even desirable. It brings back your friendship, shared humanity, and interest in one another. It deepens your bond and, at the same time, keeps you from becoming upset over little things. It enhances your perspective as well as your sense of humor. A question we often ask ourselves and each other is this: "What's wrong with being human, anyway?" Presumably, that's why we're here—to experience being human, to grow, to become more spiritual, to love, and to learn.

61.

MAKE PEACE WITH CHANGE

It's been said that there are only two certainties in life—death and taxes. Not true. A third certainty, one that is constant and must be dealt with on a day-to-day, moment-to-moment basis, is change. And one of the greatest gifts you can give yourself and your relationship is to be at peace with this fact of life.

Although we often wish it were otherwise, nothing stays the same. Our bodies change, as does our health. We can fight it, but change continues. Our moods change, almost constantly, as do our perceptions. One moment we feel inspired and loving—then, out of the blue, we experience doubt or fear. A few hours later, we're back on track.

Our relationship is always changing as well. One day, our partner says something really nice and everything seems fine. We feel grateful to be in our relationship. Other days, our partner says something wrong or fails to live up to an expectation. We become furious and may even wonder why we are with our partner.

When you resist change, you're never more than a moment away from disappointment. Whether you know it or not, you're always on guard because you're either trying to keep things the same if you like what you're experiencing—or you're fighting to make things different.

There is tremendous freedom that comes with the acceptance of change.

Embracing change means that you stop demanding that life be other than it really is in this moment. For example, rather than becoming despondent or annoyed when your partner says the wrong thing, makes a mistake, or is crabby or irritable, you are able to take it in stride. You know that this will happen thousands of times during the course of your relationship. And that's okay, because you also know that the good times and the good feelings will return. In other words, you enjoy and cherish the good times, the happy moments, but you don't hold onto them too tightly. You know that nothing lasts forever—including the wonderful feelings that exist when everything is just right. You treasure your shared laughter and your mutual feelings of closeness, but when the mood changes, you don't lose your perspective—or your love for your partner.

So many popular love songs include messages like "Things will never change," "I'll always feel this way for you," "I will always love you just like this," or "Make this moment last forever." It's sung in many different (often beautiful) ways, but the essence is the hope and dream that those passionate and loving feelings will always remain.

It seems to us that one of the reasons many people become so dissatisfied with their relationship is for just this reason. They do feel love for someone, and it's wonderful. But when the feelings change or shift, panic or at least disappointment sets in. There is a sense that "Hey, this isn't the way I want things to be," or "Things are different. That wasn't supposed to happen." As a result, they either become very unhappy and settle for that state of mind, or they begin to look for someone else.

It doesn't have to be like that. When you embrace rather than resist change, you begin to accept and usually enjoy each moment as it arises. You spend less energy judging the moment and demanding that it be different— e.g., "I don't like this"—and more energy simply experiencing it. You begin to understand that your relationship is a series of moments—tens of thousands of them—and those moments are constantly changing. Many will be happy moments and others will not. This doesn't mean you don't prefer the happy ones—we all do—only that you're not willing to fight a losing battle.

You can imagine how much more at ease your partner will become when he or she feels loved and accepted all the time, instead of only when he or she is behaving according to your plan! There's no question about it, the acceptance of change will bring peace and harmony into every aspect of your relationship.

62.

DON'T OVERANALYZE
THE FLAWS

♥ In Stategy #61, we referred to the fact that there are a few certainties in life—death and taxes among them. There is at least one additional item, however, that can be added to this very short list of certainties: If you overanalyze the flaws of your partner, you will be successful in identifying them. You'll be able to convince yourself that your partner has some serious work to do! In other words, if you look carefully enough, you will succeed in validating the fact that your partner—the person you love—is riddled with flaws. Invariably, your clever detective work will lead to serious doubts and resentments regarding your relationship. The more you analyze, the more likely it will be that you'll fall into the "analysis paralysis" trap—the tendency to overuse your thinking.

The problem with this almost insidious tendency is that it virtually guarantees that your relationship will suffer. Let's face it. Most of us are pretty bright individuals. When we look for something—i.e., think about it enough—we will almost always find and validate what we're looking for.

We've known people over the years who felt their relationship was basically very solid and loving. They decided, however, that seeing a good therapist or marriage counselor might be a good idea to help them grow together. What happened, however, was that the therapist encouraged them to analyze and ponder their "issues." They did, and almost ended up divorced.

Please don't misunderstand me; I have nothing against therapists. In fact, many are friends of mine whom I respect greatly. There are many times when therapy can be enormously helpful and, in fact, can often save marriages or struggling relationships. However, the one aspect of counseling that you may want to be cautious about is the tendency to overanalyze things that are bothering you. You'll notice, if you reflect carefully, that whenever you overanalyze anything that bothers you, you'll end up a little discouraged, frustrated, or angry. At an absolute minimum, you'll be sweating the small stuff—big time! I think you'll agree that these are not feelings that are ideally suited to bring forth greater love in your relationship.

The next time you find yourself overanalyzing your relationship, see if you can back off—just a little. Ask yourself the question, "Am I really upset about my partner—or is the fact that I'm totally caught up in my thinking contributing to my unloving feelings?" You may be amazed at what you discover! As you back off of your analytical thinking—even a little bit—your irritation will begin to diminish and your love will return. You'll discover that if something is truly significant, it will still be there to discuss and think about after you've given it a fair chance to dissolve. So, our suggestion is this: Stop overanalyzing your partner's flaws, and there will be fewer to contend with.

63.

CHOOSE TO BE SUPPORTIVE

(KRIS)

Every relationship will have its share of ups and downs. We all know that life is easiest when things are going well. We also know that it's a different story when times are tough. You can keep the inevitable downs from spiraling ever further downward, however, by choosing to be supportive.

Trish and Gavin had been married for ten years when, quite unexpectedly, Gavin lost his job. They lived in a town where it was highly improbable that he would be able to work in the same industry, at even close to the same pay scale. With two young children and a hefty mortgage, there was genuine cause for alarm.

The way Trish handled this crisis was so courageous and filled with wisdom that we felt we had to share it with you. Scary as it was (and it really was), she made the decision to remain supportive. Rather than complain or belittle Gavin in even the slightest way, she made it perfectly clear that she would do whatever was necessary to support him in his efforts. She made it clear that she believed in him, regardless of what had happened or what they might face in the future. She didn't blame him or attempt to make him feel bad. She didn't complain to her friends or compare their situation to anyone else. She was perfectly willing to move from the home she loved, go back to work, or live a much reduced lifestyle. Any or all of the above were perfectly fine with her. Rather than focusing on what was wrong, she remained grateful for all that they did have. She became a pillar of strength and an example of what's good in a relationship.

While many people may also have responded to such a crisis by being supportive, what made her response so unique was her uplifting attitude. She wasn't being supportive with a hint of resentment. Rather, her support was genuine and from the heart. It wasn't "put-on"; it was real.

Resentment and other forms of negativity are easy to embrace during difficult times. How easy, for example, it would have been to feel sorry for herself, or to make little jabbing comments indicating her displeasure.

To make a long story short, the two of them did have to sell their home and move to a new city. Rather than tearing them apart, however, it became an adventure that strengthened their commitment and their love for one another. Gavin ended up changing careers and, for a while, their finances were extremely tight. In time, however, their situation improved.

There is no doubt that Gavin will remember Trish's support for as long as they live. When he speaks about her, it's with enormous respect and gratitude. I doubt very seriously that this would have been the case had her response been more typical.

We can all learn from their experience and the way Trish handled herself—Richard and I certainly have. It's obvious that her reaction enabled him to stay focused on helping to solve their predicament rather than on feeling bad about himself. Also reinforced was the idea that we don't always have control over our destiny—but we do have some control over the way we choose to respond to adversity. Again, we are reminded that circumstances don't make a couple; they reveal them. Trish was revealed as a partner who chooses to be supportive. It worked for them and can work for you.

64.

JUMP AHEAD AND LOOK BACK

One day we were sitting together at lunch when Kris posed the question, "Someday, when we look back on our lives together, I wonder what we will remember most and what will have been most important." The more we thought about our answers, it became clear to us that the question itself is an important one. Since that time, we've known many couples who have engaged in the same mental exercise and, so far, everyone seems to agree that it's both interesting and helpful.

Somehow, everything appears clearer and substantially less urgent when looked at from a distance. With enough time, you're somehow able to put things in perspective and to differentiate between what's truly relevant and what only seems relevant at the moment. As you imagine looking back over your life, it's as though you are depersonalizing your experience, as if to see it more objectively.

I remember thinking how much we would probably emphasize the good times over the bad and our positive experiences over the negative. Kris correctly pointed out how often we have already looked back at what was difficult or painful and, in retrospect, we point to those experiences as being among the most important for personal growth and a rich experience of life. For example, had we not almost been killed in a car accident, we might not have had the same appreciation for the gift of life. Had we not struggled financially and made some stupid investments while we were young, we couldn't possibly have fully appreciated the luxury of having enough, or the importance of giving back to those less fortunate than ourselves. Had we not experienced physical pain, we wouldn't appreciate the importance of taking care of ourselves, nor would we have been able to appreciate the gift of being without pain. Had we not lost good friends, forever, to drunk drivers, we may never have appreciated the importance of slowing down enough to enjoy each precious day and to recognize that, yes, bad things can happen to good people.

Kris wondered what other gifts, disguised as painful experiences, we would look back on later on, down the road. She chuckled as she said, "I know for sure that we won't look back and say, 'If only those daily little hassles hadn't happened, we would have been so much happier.'" To the contrary, we realized that, in the end, most of the things that so trouble most of us will be remembered as completely irrelevant, if they are remembered at all. Any and all bickering or arguing, or need to prove ourselves, will be seen for what it is—a sad waste of time and energy.

What will be most relevant to us is the love that we were able to share with each other and with other people, the incredible gift of our two children and the joy they brought to our lives, and any spiritual growth and insights we were able to experience in our short journey here on earth.

We agreed that what would seem most unimportant were our minor frustrations with each other, our obsession with achievement, our concerns over things like our weight, physical appearance, the home we lived in and how clean it was, material possessions, or the size of our bank account. It's not that these things, and so many things like them, aren't important to a good life—it's just that they are less significant than other things.

Other couples point to similar insights as they practice this exercise. Friends have said, in the midst of a difficult time, "I'll bet even this, as painful as it seems, will be insignificant as we look back on it. Why don't we make the decision to drop our frustration now?" It's increased perspective like this that enables couples to stop sweating the small stuff and to start focusing on more important things.

That's what this strategy is all about—learning to drop things that you know in your heart aren't worth fretting about. After all, if you know something is going to seem meaningless at a later date, why not make it meaningless now?

We encourage you take some time and reflect on this exercise. Go on and jump ahead in your mind to the end of your life. Now look back and observe what you see. With any luck, you'll notice a thing or two you might consider changing—a priority, a habit, a self-defeating belief, or an attitude about life. At worst, you'll find this to be an interesting exercise. At best, it will change the way you look at things.

65.

REMEMBER THE EQUATION:
A HAPPY PERSON EQUALS
A HAPPY PARTNER

Sometimes, the most obvious equations are the most overlooked. You know, things like "If you want to feel good, you have to take care of yourself." Obvious? Sure, but how many of us really do? Or, "If you spend too much money on your credit card over the holidays, you'll regret it in January." Again, pretty obvious, but most of us do it anyway.

This strategy falls into this category. For whatever reasons, we often choose personal convenience or some other selfish reaction over attempting to look after the happiness of our partner. Yet, doing so violates a clear equation—a happy person equals a happy partner—and pretty much guarantees unnecessary stress and strife in your relationship.

We are certainly of the mindset that it's not your responsibility to make your partner happy. In fact, there's an entire strategy in this book dedicated to the idea that we all must take responsibility for our own happiness. Yet, there are things all of us can do—little things, no-brainers—that clearly contribute to our partner's happiness. And when your partner is happy, he or she is almost always easier to be with. A happy person is also more likely to be a better listener and a more passionate lover, more inclined to share in the joy of others, more giving and compassionate, and more likely to make decisions that enhance the quality of a relationship.

So what's the catch?

The catch is that, occasionally, it's inconvenient to make decisions that make your partner happy. Or it requires a little sacrifice. Or it makes you a little uncomfortable. But in the end, it's almost always worth it. Not only do you get to see your partner happy, but it's nourishing to your relationship as well.

For example, it's inconvenient for Kris to encourage me to spend time alone—particularly because I already travel a great deal on business. When I'm gone, it means more work for her. So why does she encourage it, when so many other men and women would discourage it, or at least complain about it? The answer is that, in addition to simply being thoughtful, she knows that it brings me joy to spend time alone. And when I'm happier, I'm a better husband and father. I'm more fun, lighthearted, and helpful, and I'm more relaxed and patient.

I try to give Kris the same respect and encouragement in return. It's by no means convenient, yet, if she wants to go out of town to visit friends, or whatever, I try to be as encouraging as possible. I can't imagine complaining about something that would make her happy. In addition, Kris loves horses and enjoys spending time around them whenever possible. Despite not being a horse lover, I've tried over the years not only to accommodate her wishes, but to be encouraging, helpful, and supportive as well. In fact, one of my daily chores is shoveling horse manure! I certainly don't *have* to be supportive— nor does Kris. But why wouldn't we? We go back and forth, trying whenever possible to make decisions geared toward each other's happiness. We don't always put each other first, but, on balance, we do a pretty good job.

Maybe your partner has special hobbies or interests that take some of her time and energy. Or maybe she belongs to a club or organization apart from you. Perhaps he likes to watch sports with his friends or to smoke cigars. Or she might have special friends that she likes to visit or talk with on the phone. Perhaps she loves to exercise early in the morning, requiring you to get more involved in the early-morning routine around the house. It could be any of these things or something else altogether. Whatever it is, it might require some accommodation, compromise, or sacrifice on your part. If so, don't sweat it! If it makes her happier, it's probably worth it.

66.

ASK FOR "DREAM UPDATES"

♥ Are you aware of your partner's dreams—what he or she really wants out of life? Do you know what her secret fantasies are—what she sees herself doing, her ideal life, what would make her feel complete? Are you sure? Or are you simply assuming that you know? Have you asked? If so, when was the last time?

It seems to us that many people have virtually no idea, beyond the superficial, of what their partner's personal dreams really are. Sure, most people are able to say things like, "He wants financial security," or "She wants to be a mother." But beyond these almost universal preferences, an awareness—or sense of caring—for a partner's dreams seems to stop. This tendency seems to increase in direct proportion to the length of a relationship. When you first fall in love, you zero in on your partner's dreams. As time goes by, however, they fade into the background, until at some point they all but disappear.

Obviously there are many aspects to a relationship. From the perspective of feeling connected, however, one of the most enjoyable and nourishing is the sharing—back and forth—of dreams. There is something so rich and pleasurable about telling someone your vision, what you'd like to do, where you would like to go, and the contributions you'd like to make. And when the person you're sharing with is "right there with you," sharing your dreams, truly listening with interest and respect, your dreams come alive and your shared experience can be almost magical. There's no question that this type of interaction helps to connect two people. And, luckily, it can also help to reconnect two people who may have lost sight of their partner's dreams.

Over the years, we've spoken to dozens of people who have had extramarital affairs, left or divorced their spouse, or simply lost interest in the relationship altogether. When asked the question, "Why do you think it happened?" in almost every instance, the person included in their answer, "The (new) person listened to me—he (or she) was genuinely interested in my dreams, and in what I had to say."

In no way are we excusing unfaithful behavior or placing the blame on a spouse or partner who has been faithful. To do so would be irresponsible. We are, however, attempting to point out how powerful the need to be "heard" and listened to really is. And, as importantly, how destructive it is when this need isn't being met.

When a person feels comfortable sharing their dreams—when they are asked to share them—there is a degree of safety, satisfaction, and aliveness that is felt and experienced. Conversely, when a person doesn't feel comfortable sharing her dreams—when she is never asked—there is often a feeling that something is missing.

The idea of asking for dream updates is a powerful strategy because whether or not the dream comes true is less relevant than the fact that your partner knows and cares what you want. Let's face reality: None of us can have everything we want. Yet, it's really nice to be able to share our dreams—and to know that someone else shares them with us.

Asking for dream updates can bring the magic back to your relationship. Everyone loves to share his or her dreams. So, starting today, make it a point to ask your partner for a dream update. You'll be contributing to making her dreams come true.

67.

NEVER UNDERESTIMATE
THE POWER OF LOVE

♥ Years ago, I was at a relationship seminar when a member of the audience stood up and asked the speaker, "Why should I act loving to my wife? She doesn't act loving to me!" The speaker responded in a gentle and nonjudgmental manner, "Because you need the practice."

His words hit me like a ton of bricks and have always stuck with me. His advice was, and still is, right on the mark. In fact, I can't think of a single person who doesn't need more practice in the art of acting loving. Can you? Do you know people who have mastered the art of loving kindness? If so, I'd love to meet them.

With rare exception, we all need practice in unconditional love. We can all stand to be less defensive, selfish, and reactive. Most of us would be better off if we were better listeners, kinder, gentler, and a little more generous. But to embrace these qualities requires practice—not so much when our partner is acting loving and supportive, but rather, during those times when he or she is off-track and acting unloving. In other words, it's easy to be kind and loving when our partner is already doing so. It's something else altogether to do so when they are not.

You can transform your relationship forever by utilizing the power of love. If you can respond with love instead of reacting with frustration—if you can remain loving instead of acting defensive—and if you can keep your heart open, even when it seems uncalled-for, you will have discovered the power of love and the most effective way to ensure lasting and nourishing relationships in your life.

To fully utilize the power of love is certainly easier said than done. However, it's not as difficult as you might think. All that is required is your intention to do so, along with—you guessed it—plenty of practice. When your partner is being attentive and loving, enjoy and appreciate it. But when she is not, that is the time to turn your heart to the "on" position. Rather than insist that she act differently, do your best to be understanding and unconditionally loving. Let it go. Be forgiving and listen well. Keep your sense of humor and be supportive.

One of the most mysterious and magical qualities of all relationships is the interconnectedness that develops between two people. When your heart is full of anger, chances are your relationship will suffer. When you are demanding and aggressive, your partner will tend to close down. When your mind is filled with thoughts about what's not right with your partner, and other forms of mental negativity, your partner will, in some way, sense your ill feelings and remain distant and guarded. Your relationship will not be all that it can be—not even close.

On the other hand, in most cases, when your heart is filled with love, your partner will feel that too! Her defenses will drop and she will usually return to a more loving feeling. When your partner says or does something "wrong" and you can brush it off and remain loving, he or she will bounce back more quickly than if you react with harsh thoughts of retaliation. If you can maintain an inner environment of love, relatively undistracted by less than perfect behavior, most issues will quickly resolve themselves. I'm not referring to burying your head in the sand or putting up with abusive behavior, but rather learning to let go of the little things so that your heart can remain open.

The next time you find yourself feeling agitated or annoyed at your partner, try a different strategy. Rather than continuing the typical and virtually universal cycle of demanding that he or she be the first to change, be open to the possibility of acting loving in spite of it all. You may be quite surprised at how quickly and dramatically things will turn for the better. Never underestimate the power of love.

68.

DON'T LET YOUR CHILDREN
COME BETWEEN YOU

♥ I believe that Kris and I have done a remarkable job in this category. We love our children more than words can say—we adore them, want the best for them, and, to a large degree, have dedicated our lives to them. They make our lives complete and there is no question that they are our top priority.

Yet, we love each other too. A ton! And we don't just say this—we mean it. We're great pals and best friends. We love to spend time together—to share, laugh, love one another, be silly, hang out, or just be quiet. We're partners.

We decided long ago that nothing—not even our children—would ever come between us. Furthermore, we realized, early on, that one of the most important messages we could give our children was to set an example as two parents who truly love *and* like each other; two people who prioritize one another and look forward to being together—even though we have a family to nurture and care for.

It appears to have worked really well. Both our children know how we feel about each other. They realize, on a deep level, that we have a mutual respect and admiration for each other, that we stick up for one another, agree on most fronts, and, most of all, that we love each other. There is no question in either of their minds. In fact, it's so clear to both of them that, when Saturday morning rolls around, one of them will usually say something like, "Where are you guys going tonight?" or "Who gets to babysit us tonight?" They assume we are going to go somewhere together because they know it's important to us—just as it's important for them to spend time with their best friends. To them, it would seem bizarre if we didn't.

Every set of parents is obviously different and will have different values and degrees of comfort where this issue is concerned. Our goal isn't to get other parents to prioritize their lives as we have. Yet, for us, we are positive that we are doing the right thing, not only for our relationship, but for our kids as well. Our guess is that their expectations regarding their boyfriends and future husbands will be fairly high. Our hope is that they will eventually seek partners who value not only their children (if they have them), but their relationships as well. We know many parents who, even years after having children, rarely go out alone—and a few who never have. It has always seemed to us that, even if you didn't like each other very much and if your only goal was to send a good message to your children about relationships—then you'd prioritize your relationship, at least once in a while. Otherwise, it would seem, they would grow up believing a "normal" relationship neither requires nor deserves any time or effort—the relationship would be seen as secondary, if not dispensable.

It's been said millions of times before—but worth repeating one more time: If you want a loving relationship, you must prioritize it and treat it as important. The truth is, you vote with your actions. You can say, "My marriage is really important," but your actions may be saying something entirely different. You may virtually never spend time alone with your spouse, or go out alone with her. Hardly the way you would behave if your goal was to appear loving. After all, you spend time with the kids and as a family, and you spend time at work, doing chores, shopping for "stuff," and in front of the television—so why not with your so-called loved one? Is that what you would hope for with your child—that he or she would grow up and never, ever spend time alone with their spouse, once they had children?

Finally, when you spend time together, even though you have children, you send a powerful message to one another that each of you matters, and so does your relationship. It's harder to sweat the small stuff with your partner when you both know that you are important to the other. So, however you do it, and to whatever degree, consider the importance of putting your relationship first. If you do, everyone wins.

69.

LEARN TO DEFLECT OCCASIONAL
UNCALLED-FOR COMMENTS

♥ There doesn't seem to be any way to get through life without saying some pretty stupid things. Unless you are unique, you're going to slip up every once in a while—when you're tired, insecure, grumpy, or just in an old-fashioned bad mood. Every once in a while, regardless of how nice a person you are or how pure your intentions, you're likely to say something insensitive, condescending, arrogant, mean-spirited, or just plain uncalled-for. You might come across as judgmental, reactive; or you might say something about someone's appearance or intelligence. Or you're going to lecture someone inappropriately or come across as ignorant or petty. Probably all of the above. The fact is, you're human.

But so is your partner! And humans make mistakes.

If you can make allowances for the fact that your partner, like you, is going to mess up every once in a while, you'll have an edge that very few seem to enjoy. What's more, your accepting attitude will virtually guarantee that the number of times this happens will be minimal. Your lack of insistence that your partner be flawless will create an emotional environment that will bring out the best in him. He won't feel like he has to walk around on eggshells, or as though you are keeping score of his behavior. When someone doesn't feel pressured to be perfect, the most common response is to lighten up, open the heart, and act more loving.

Okay, you're in a relationship. Your partner is tired and in a bad mood. He says something stupid or inappropriate. Every time this happens, you're at a fork in the road. You can, of course (like most do), react. You can snap back or in some other way defend yourself. You can fill your head with anger or hostility and feel angry and resentful. You can think of all the times your partner has done the same thing and feel sorry for yourself. You can even slam the door and call a friend to talk about it.

Or you can roll your eyes and accept the fact that all of us say and do things, every once in a while, that we shouldn't. Period, end of subject. You can simply let it go and remain loving.

Either way, the comment has already been made. It may as well be ancient history because it can't be taken back. This is a new moment, a new opportunity to remain loving.

Consider how the two responses are received by your partner. He's already been insensitive. Now it's your turn. Do you compound the problem by proving that you can't handle it—that you can't love unconditionally either? Or do you try to set a better example? Can you try to use love, rather than revenge, as the solution? We think you'll find that love is the most powerful remedy to almost all minor day-to-day issues, including this one. So much so that when you don't react to the comment—but instead remain loving—you'll often find your partner laughing at himself, if not apologizing for his behavior.

Obviously, we are referring to a normally healthy and loving relationship and the way we respond to an *occasional* slip of the tongue or uncalled-for comment. We're not talking here about excusing abusive behavior or *patterns* of negative behavior. That's a totally different story.

So the next time it happens, try this new way of responding—or not responding, as the case may be. You may find that it's easier than you imagine to begin thinking of occasional uncalled-for comments as "small stuff" rather than as such a big deal. And, as such, you can let it go and get on with being in love.

70.

DON'T COME HOME
FRAZZLED

♥ This is a simple but dramatic way to make your interactions more peaceful after a long and tiring day. In many cases, it can help you become more patient and understanding, while making that often-difficult transition between work and home a whole lot easier. On a day-to-day basis, it can help you reconnect to the one you love, reminding you why you are together to begin with.

It's extremely common for one (sometimes both) partners in a relationship to enter the home after a long day at work as if he or she were crossing the finish line of a race. The frenetic, hectic pace at work is brought into the home. Without even knowing it, you may be storming into the house still revved and charged from the rest of the day.

Common sense will tell you that when you are speeded up, frantic, and hurried, you lose many of your most desirable human traits—patience, listening skills, perspective, wisdom, a sense of peace, and your ability to be genuinely loving. When you're in a frantic state of mind, you are more easily agitated, annoyed, and bothered. Without even knowing it, you can be demanding, and your expectations may become elevated. Almost always, you'll be more reactive, and things will tend to get to you very easily—especially small things. Consequently, as you and your partner engage in conversation and come together for the evening, you'll be less inclined to be fully attentive and "present." You may be a bit distracted and, without question, things will get to you that normally wouldn't seem to be a very big deal.

The solution is quite simple and may take only a few minutes. Before you come home, stop your car and get out. Take a few minutes to unwind, slow down, breathe, and relax your body. Gently remind yourself that your workday is over and it's time to change gears, to slow down. If you have a park bench you can sit in or a place to watch the sunset or observe nature, that works great, but isn't critical. What's most important is the conscious acknowledgment that it's in your best interest to be able to slow down and relax. Not only will you feel better, but your partner will appreciate the difference in you as well. Let's be realistic here. Very few people appreciate someone—regardless of how much they love that person—who barges in and stirs things up.

We know a couple who integrated a variation of this strategy that virtually saved their marriage. The husband was a poster boy for the tendency we're describing. He would, with good intentions, walk in the door and immediately begin firing questions and explaining his own difficult day. He was so speeded-up that he would become impatient with the relatively calm demeanor of his wife. She couldn't stand what she called the "nervous energy" of her husband. It was the time of day when she was beginning to feel a little relaxed, and his presence would essentially ruin her evening. It got to the point where she would dread his return from work.

They went to a marriage counselor who came up with a brilliant solution. She instructed the husband to walk in the back door, rather than the front door when returning from work. He was to go straight to the bath for a fifteen-minute, relaxing soak. This did two things. First, it genuinely helped him to relax, both his body and his mind. But, more importantly, it reminded him that his "hurried reality" was not shared by his wife. She so much appreciated this simple effort that she became far less reactive herself when he would revert to his old ways.

Eventually, this became a nonissue for this couple. He slowed down and she stopped caring so much. Today, they are as happy as any two people can be. Obviously, this strategy will have relative importance depending on how speeded-up either one of you—or both—has become. Yet, we hope you won't underestimate the importance of not coming home in a heated rush. Making that transition from work to home a slower one can pay enormous dividends in your relationship.

71.

ASK YOUR PARTNER THE QUESTION, "WHAT'S THE MOST DIFFICULT PART OF BEING IN A RELATIONSHIP WITH ME?"

It's understandable that, for many people, this can be a somewhat frightening experience. The fear, of course, lies in discovering what you might find out—or what your partner might say to you, given the permission to speak his or her mind. Obviously, you may already know, or at least have a really strong suspicion of what bugs your partner, so the answer may not be much of a surprise. However, asking the question is entirely different from receiving unsolicited lectures or requests from your partner.

Clearly, this strategy does require an openness as well as some degree of courage and humility. However, despite any initial discomfort you may feel, it's almost always worth the effort, and won't be nearly as difficult as you imagine it to be. Instead, the question tends to bring forth openness, insightful communication, and ultimately a feeling of gratitude. After all, almost everyone appreciates a partner who is actively trying to improve the relationship.

This is a true shortcut to a better relationship. It's important to acknowledge the fact that, whether or not you choose to ask this question, there *are* things about you that bug your partner. In other words, either way, the issue is there—either silently or out in the open. You can try to keep it buried—but usually that creates resentment. In other words, if you remain silent, your partner is still going to have to live with whatever it is that bugs her. If you ask the question, then at least you'll know what it is that bugs her, and you'll have the opportunity to make an adjustment.

It's interesting to observe what happens to another person's dissatisfaction when you allow, even encourage, them the privilege of getting whatever it is that concerns them off their chest. Often, when you sincerely and nondefensively want to know the answer, it will take the edge or "sting" off of the issue. When you are willing to look at your issues instead of resisting or denying them, your partner will sense your sincere desire to work toward positive change. He or she will, in turn, tend to become less defensive and reactive around the issue, and will often be able to discuss the subject in an unheated, even loving manner. In other words, it will be harder for them to "sweat" what's bothering them when they are aware of your efforts to curb it.

Several years ago, Kris and I were walking hand in hand through a beautiful beach town in northern California. The feeling between us was loving, and I was feeling secure. That was the first time that it had ever occurred to me to ask this question—and I did. To my delight, Kris thought it was a "sweet" thing to ask. After reflecting for a few moments, she said to me, "Do you know what really bugs me about you?" She paused for a moment and then continued. "You're really difficult to be around the day you pay your bills." She went on to say, in effect, that I get short-tempered and easily bothered, and I feel sorry for myself just about every time I sit down to write a check.

I was relieved to know that, of the thousands of things she probably could have said, she choose something relatively minor! Nevertheless, because I genuinely wanted to know what bothered her about me, it was easy to accept and I could see exactly what she meant. As I thought about it, it was clear that my entire personality would go through a negative transformation each time I sat down to pay my bills. Without feeling the slightest bit defensive, I thanked her for sharing with me and made a silent commitment to be more aware of this tendency in the future.

Again, it's obvious that this was a relatively minor issue. However, Kris had brought to my attention something that was completely invisible to me—my reaction to paying bills had become a bad habit that was adversely affecting the way she felt around me. I was sweating the small stuff. I had no idea that my entire personality and mood would change before, during, and after paying bills—but she was absolutely right. Because I now knew how this issue was affecting her, it was relatively easy over the ensuing months to make an adjustment in my attitude and to make life around our home a little more peaceful during bill-paying times.

We encourage you to experiment with this strategy. Your partner may share with you something minor, or something more serious. Either way, you'll get it out in the open in a nondefensive environment and you'll have the chance to make whatever it is a "nonissue." If all goes well, perhaps your partner may even ask you for your feedback, as well. If that turns out not to be the case, however, that's okay too. Whatever you do, don't demand reciprocation. If you do, your partner will probably have one more issue to discuss with you next time you ask this question.

72.

DON'T QUESTION HER
(OR HIS) MOTIVES

For many of us, one of the nicest things about growing up is that you are free, within reason, to make your own decisions. There is something so nourishing and rewarding about making a decision, feeling good about it, and feeling supported, or at least "unhassled" about that decision. For example, if you decide, "I'd like to spend a day this next weekend alone," it's rewarding and reinforces the joy of the decision if that decision is honored by your partner. The same is true whether your decision has to do with something you want to do or something you've already done; a dream or a plan that you're pursuing; a course you wish to take; a direction you're headed; a hobby you wish to pursue; the dish you've decided to prepare for dinner; or practically anything else.

It's something else, altogether, however, if you have to explain or defend your decision. If your partner says, "Why do you have to do that?" or "Shouldn't you be spending your time doing something different?" having to explain yourself takes the wind out of your sails—and your plans. It turns something satisfying into something stressful. Instead of feeling unconditionally supported, you feel as though you're on trial.

We were at the beach when I overheard a woman telling her husband she was going to have lunch with an old girlfriend. His response speaks to the essence of this strategy. In a condescending tone he said, "Why are you going to spend your time with her?" It was obvious that he disapproved and was questioning her motives. As you might guess, she began defending her decision. In a matter of seconds, they went from having a quiet, relaxing afternoon on the beach to having a stressful and highly defensive interaction, most likely ruining the remainder of their day. Quite frankly, it was awful even being around them. What makes this type of story so sad is that it's absolutely unnecessary.

Can you imagine how much more respect and love this woman would have for her husband had he simply said, "That sounds like fun," or "Good for you"? She would have felt great and probably would have continued sharing her life and her decisions with her husband. After all, it wasn't his choice—it was hers. Even if for some strange reason he didn't think it was in her best interest, so what? She had already made the decision. It was hers to live with—not his.

When you question someone's motives, especially when they are obviously innocent, you are making the statement, "I don't have enough respect for you to allow you to make your own decisions. You must clear them with me so that I can give you my approval or disapproval."

You only have to read this strategy to get the point—questioning your partners's motives on a regular basis is a surefire way to interfere with an otherwise loving relationship. Truthfully, it's an ugly quality that is never appreciated.

Obviously, an occasional questioning comment isn't going to make or break your connection. But if you're in the habit of questioning the motives of your partner, it might be a good idea to see the wisdom of breaking this habit, once and for all. Probably the best way to break it is to convince yourself of how selfish it really is. Questioning the motives of your partner sends the message that, deep down, you don't trust, respect, or approve of the decisions your partner is making. It implies that your partner isn't wise enough to make good decisions. Further, it encourages highly defensive reactions and takes much of the joy out of sharing.

Obviously, we're not talking about never questioning a motive. If something truly involves you or your relationship, or if it's really important, that's a different matter. We're talking about little, daily stuff.

We encourage you to give this strategy some serious consideration. You'll be amazed at how much more open and lighthearted your partner will become if you simply stop questioning his or her motives. Rather than questioning her motives, share in her enthusiasm. It's so enjoyable to share with someone who allows you to do so freely, without question. If you give this a try, you'll be forever glad you did.

73.

GRACIOUSLY RECEIVE
COMPLIMENTS

In an earlier strategy, we discussed the importance of dishing out regular compliments. This strategy deals with the flip side of that issue.

A number of years ago I was listening to a radio talk show when the guest, an expert on relationships, alluded to the fact that one of the saddest mistakes people make in relationships is the failure to receive compliments. This was a little surprising because most of the people I give compliments to are able to receive kind words easily and gracefully. And, for the most part, I feel pretty comfortable with this part of life as well.

Yet, because the guest on the show sounded convincing and as if he knew what he was talking about, I decided to verify his comments for myself. I started by asking people—both compliment givers and compliment receivers. Both groups of people overwhelmingly supported the expert's conclusion that, in reality, most of us are really bad when it comes to receiving a compliment. Over the past decade, I've listened to many people receive compliments and in doing so, I, too, have come to the same conclusion.

I'm not sure exactly what it is. Some of us feel a little shy, awkward, or embarrassed when someone gives us a compliment. We might respond by lowering our head, blushing, or saying something to minimize the kind words. For example, when someone says, "You're really good at that," you might say something like, "Not really," or "I'm not as good as you think." Or you'll give some explanation to downplay the compliment: "I got really lucky," or "I only won because the other person was sick."

Another way we sometimes deflect a compliment is to turn it around—as if to make the compliment about the other person. So, in response to the statement, "You look really nice today," you might say, "Not as nice as you."

On the surface, responding to compliments in ways such as these would seem harmless. After all, you're being humble and humility is certainly a wonderful quality. When you take a closer look, however, you'll notice that while you are indeed being humble and certainly intending no harm, you are not being very gracious. In fact, responding to compliments in this way can be a little insulting and might even hurt the feelings of the compliment giver.

It takes thoughtfulness, courage, and kindness to give someone a genuine, heartfelt compliment. So, when someone rejects your compliment, however unintentionally, it hurts. And while it's not so horrible that your partner is likely to say anything, it's nevertheless a little deflating. It sends the wrong kind of silent message. Instead of affirming your appreciation to your partner and acknowledging the gesture in a positive way, it either says, "You're wrong," or "I don't really deserve the compliment." Either way, it's a bit of a putdown.

Remember, it's fun to dish out compliments. When you're excited or proud about something your partner has done, it's rewarding to share your enthusiasm. When you aren't gracious, however, you rob your partner of that enjoyment. Instead of encouraging further compliments, you reduce the likelihood because you've taken the fun out of the giving.

This is an easy problem to solve. The trick is to think less about what the compliment says about you—and more about what it means to the person giving it to you. When you do, you'll probably find it much easier and more natural to graciously receive your compliments.

74.

LET GO OF YOUR TOP
THREE PET PEEVES

For years, as a way of gathering information, we've been asking the question, "What is it that bugs you the most about your partner?" While the details are usually different from person to person, there are two broad themes that stand out. First, more often than not, what bugs people are the little things—those annoying little quirks and habits. Second, on average, there seem to be about three primary pet peeves per person. Time and time again, people tell us, "Our relationship would be so much better if my partner would stop doing these three things."

As far as we can tell, there are only two ways to overcome this reality. The first is pure fantasy—thinking that your partner is going to be able and willing to change. But the other way is creative and incredibly effective—to choose to let go of your top three pet peeves.

This sounds harder than it actually is. When you examine your options, you'll discover that this is indeed your best and only reasonable course of action. You'll see that the reason pet peeves bug you is that you allow them to bug you—you give them too much attention. Because you've always demanded (or hoped) that they would disappear, you've related to them as an enemy, giving them far too much mental energy and significance. Once you surrender to the fact that they aren't going to go away and you decide to make peace with them, you will be able to see the innocence in them and, in many instances, the humor in them.

One of my previous pet peeves with Kris was that she frequently forgot to turn off her closet light. It's a stupid little thing that used to drive me nuts! My reasons for being upset always seemed to make sense—the ceiling is high, and I'm the one who has to change the bulb. But for whatever reason, I would walk by and the light was always on. I'd complain about it, remind her, make gentle little hints, and have plenty of conversations in my head about the habit—but to no avail. I'd walk by the next time and the light would be on again.

Then one day it hit me. If this was all I had to complain about Kris— I'm one really lucky guy! God knows, I have many habits far more bothersome than this one. I decided to make peace with the fact that the issue was really mine and that it was not worth holding onto. Turning a light switch to the off position is a ridiculous thing to spend any amount of energy complaining about. It takes a fraction of a second—and I probably turn off dozens of lights a day anyway. I started asking myself, "Why am I sweating this one?" Once I put it into proper perspective, it looked totally different. After all, how uptight would a person (me) have to be to get stressed out over something so minor? What I realized was that my being upset over something so benign said far more about me (and my tendency to sweat the small stuff) than it did about Kris. When you think about overreacting to pet peeves, this is almost always a fair assumption.

To this day, I continue to turn off the closet light whenever it has been left on. The difference is, I think about it differently. If anything, it's kind of cute and I either chuckle or smile when doing so. I hope you'll agree that choosing to let go of your top three pet peeves is a good idea. You'll be glad you did—and so will your partner. Who knows, perhaps your partner will let go of something irritating about you!

75.

AVOID ABSOLUTE STATEMENTS
(OF A NEGATIVE NATURE)

When we've asked people what bugs them most about their partner, a consistent reply has to do with what might be called "absolute statements." These harsh statements tend to put people into a box, paint them into a corner by defining them in an extremely narrow way. You'll probably agree that, by and large, most people don't appreciate being labeled in absolute ways. It comes across as unfair and judgmental. In fact, many consider it to be quite insulting. The only exception to this rule, of course, is when the statement is of a positive nature. For example, if you say to your partner, "You're always so thoughtful," this is obviously a different story—a positive version of an absolute statement.

Absolute statements are those that use words like "always, never, worthless, nothing," and so forth. Examples of absolute statements include, "You always say the wrong thing," "You always come home too late," "You never spend any time with the kids," "You never listen to my words," "Your contribution is worthless," "You do nothing to help," and so forth. Any statement that defines a person or explains his or her contribution in a narrow, absolute way falls into this category.

There are two very important and logical reasons to never again use these types of statements. First, as just mentioned, absolute statements can be insulting and hurtful as they are almost never accurate. We knew a man, for example, whose wife was constantly accusing him of "never" listening to her. Although, like most of the rest of us, he could improve in this area, her harsh accusations were grossly exaggerated. Both of us had seen him around her on several occasions and I can honestly say he was at least average in his listening skills. In fact, it appeared as though he may have been a better listener than she was. Furthermore, he was *genuinely* trying to be a better listener and, in fact, had taken a course in effective listening. In my view, her absolute statements were far more detrimental to their relationship than his lack of listening skills.

Think about how you would feel if your partner said to you, "You never help around the house." In all likelihood, unless you were truly a lazy slob, you'd be either hurt, annoyed, or defensive. Maybe you aren't the best house cleaner in the world, and maybe you should be more conscientious in this area, but if you are making any effort whatsoever, your partner's words will probably be received as a stab in the back, and as an untruthful jab.

The other reason it's so important not to use absolute statements is that they encourage your partner to do (or not do) the very things you are objecting to. After all, you've already shared your negative perspective with your partner, given him or her a negative and lazy reputation to live up to. So why in the world would they want to cooperate now? You're not going to give them credit, even if they do.

Once you see the compelling logic of avoiding absolute statements, the habit is relatively easy to break. If you're frustrated with your partner, a gentler and less extreme approach will almost always be better received—and will probably get you a better result. So, whenever possible, stay away from absolute statements. Doing so will serve your relationship well.

76.

PREDICT THE PREDICTABLE

♥ This strategy is helpful and practical for all couples and gets even more so the longer you have been together. It has to do with the fact that, to one degree or another, all of us have a certain amount of predictability. Happily, learning to predict the predictable—and making peace with it— can save you from a great deal of agitation.

Kris was raised in Portland, Oregon, where it rains a significant portion of the time. Most people familiar with the region would acknowledge that it would be silly to travel there (especially in the winter) and be surprised or disappointed that it was raining. You might prefer to bask in a little more sunshine, but you certainly wouldn't complain, "I can't believe it's raining— my day is ruined."

You can extend this simple wisdom to your relationship with your partner. After a while you come to expect certain responses, and you can be fairly accurate in your prediction of certain habits. Your boyfriend, for example, might become defensive every time you make plans on Sunday afternoon because that's the day he likes to watch sports on television. Once you know this, it's unnecessary, maybe even a little foolish, to take offense at his reaction. If you know what's coming, in advance, you can make certain allowances. You might decide not to make plans on Sunday. Or, if you decide to go ahead and do so anyway, you can do so compassionately, and not take his knee-jerk reaction so personally. Like the weather in Oregon, you might prefer that he cared less about watching sports, and you can certainly negotiate with him about the subject, but to become offended and upset seems a little self-defeating.

As I said before, I used to get frustrated when Kris was running even a little late. After a while, however, I learned that it was part of her nature. She becomes so immersed and enthusiastic in whatever she's doing that she has a tendency to wait a little too long to get out the door.

But once it became predictable—and I accepted it—it became a nonissue. Why make a federal case out of something so minor when it's so easy to make allowances for the predictability? I learned to bring a book, or some paperwork, or my cell phone, or I'd just be more patient, or whatever. If it was super important that she be on time, I'd just mention it, and she would make the extra effort to be on time. Whatever the issue, rather than saying, "I can't believe he or she would do that," you begin to think to yourself, "Of course he (or she) is going to do that. He always has in the past—why should this time be any different?" Again, this doesn't mean you don't care—only that you don't freak out about it.

All of us have habits, quirks, and reactions that are fairly predictable. When you let them go—instead of hassling your partner about them—you may be surprised at how often the issues fade away on their own. People change and grow, usually without our involvement. Over the years, for example, Kris has become far more punctual. In fact, today I probably run late more often than she does. It's a good thing I didn't give her too hard a time—maybe she'll be easy on me, too.

77.

STOP TREATING EVERYTHING
LIKE AN EMERGENCY

The essence of sweating the small stuff is treating life itself as if it were an emergency. Of course, there are emergencies to deal with in life—and they are always difficult. But for the most part, the ordinary, day-to-day, moment-to-moment events, challenges, interactions, and responsibilities we must attend to don't fall into this serious category.

A nourishing relationship is like a sanctuary—relaxing, comforting, and reassuring. Unfortunately, when we make a habit of turning little hassles and daily challenges into giant emergencies, we send the message to our partner that we are anything but a calming influence. Instead of being reassuring, we come across as a nervous and agitated time bomb! We are tense and agitated, and usually not very much fun to be with.

No one is calm all the time, or even close to it. However, it's important to put things into perspective and realize that many of the things we get upset and bothered by aren't really that big a deal, but rather just part of our daily lives.

One of our favorite quotes speaks so well to this issue. It comes from Alfred D. Souza. He said, "For a long time it seemed that my life was about to begin—real life. But there was always some obstacle in the way, something to be gotten through first, some unfinished business, time still to be served, a debt to be paid . . . then life would begin. At last it dawned on me that these obstacles were my life."

When we see the obstacles, even the hassles we experience, as an integral part of our life—instead of something that is getting in the way of our life—it makes virtually everything much easier to deal with. This is particularly helpful to be aware of in our relationships because it allows us to give our partner the space and freedom to be human, to make mistakes, and to occasionally say and do the wrong thing, which, as we all know, happens to all of us.

One of the greatest gifts that Kris has given to me is that she has never expected me to be even close to perfect. She's quick to forgive and almost never makes a big deal of the mistakes that I make. For the most part, she doesn't treat anything—except real emergencies—as emergencies. This makes it easy to be around her and easy to love her.

I've noticed the almost identical tendency with most of the couples I've known who have a nice, relaxed feeling between them. It's usually the case that one or both of the people don't treat ordinary things like "front-page news." Instead of freaking out or exaggerating the negative, they have a way of taking not all, but most things in stride.

Obviously, everyone has a different temperament and not everyone wants to or is capable of being calm. As a general rule, however, we've found that most people could stand to be slightly calmer and more relaxed, and perhaps a little less reactive to daily "stuff." And not always, but usually, your partner will appreciate any efforts you make toward this end.

78.

USE LETTERS AS A
COMMUNICATION TOOL

♥ Typically, when you confront someone, or when you need to have a serious discussion, it can be difficult to fully articulate your position, as well as to adequately express exactly why your position is so important to you, without your partner's becoming at least slightly defensive. Before you have fully laid out your argument, your partner is already sharing (or at least thinking about) their concerns, objections, and comebacks. This is commonly referred to as a knee-jerk reaction, and it's about as common as fur on a kitten. Sadly, most of us aren't world-class listeners.

Therefore, in certain situations, writing a letter or a card can be an appropriate and powerful way to overcome this problem. A nondefensive and "from the heart" letter can be a wonderful way to communicate a concern, preference, desire, or potential solution. The effectiveness of the letter has nothing to do with how well you write. It has everything to do with how sincerely and lovingly you can jot down your feelings.

As the writer, you have the chance to think about and describe your position slowly and carefully, without the chance of being interrupted. The recipient of the letter (your partner) has the advantage of being able to read the letter as many times as is needed in order to fully understand where you are coming from. He or she can reflect upon it, or in some instances, even cool down before offering a response.

The first time this procedure worked for us was quite by accident. Our first child was less than a year old. Kris was spending most of her time dedicated to our baby, leaving little or no time for herself. I was working, attending school, and writing my first book. We were broke and both of us were sleep deprived. We were happy and very much in love—but, like most couples with young children, a little overwhelmed.

Although I was able to get away from home on occasion, it was almost always work-related. I had tried to communicate my desire to get away alone, but the timing was always poor. Kris, even more tired than I, was unable to embrace my desire to get away. In retrospect, of course, I can see why!

One day, when she was out with our daughter, I decided to write Kris a note. In essence, this is what I said: "I love you and our family more than anything in this world. Yet, my need to be alone and have some solitude is overwhelming me. I think it would be so good for me, and ultimately us, if I could get away, even for a few days. Any suggestions?"

When I returned home that night, I had all but forgotten the note. Kris, however, had not. In fact, she said that she had read my letter several times and that she had had no idea I was so in need of time alone. Unselfishly, she encouraged me to drive to the ocean, my favorite place on earth, and spend as much time as I needed to refresh myself. She said she was sorry she hadn't thought of it before and wondered why I hadn't discussed it with her.

Remember, from my perspective, I had tried to discuss the issue many times. However, with a crying baby girl and too many responsibilities to attend to, we were never able to discuss just how important this issue was to my sanity. What the letter did was to open and expand the dialogue for a topic that was difficult for me to discuss. Without it, I may not ever have been able to express my need so clearly.

Letters such as this are not intended to be a substitute for honest and courageous communication. Instead, they are best used to open the door to relationship-deepening communication or to complement the interactions you are already having.

We've met couples who have used similar types of letters to bring up a variety of issues—a concern about overspending, a differing perspective regarding disciplining the kids, or a frustration about an unfair distribution of chores.

We've found that it's sometimes helpful to see your partner's position in black and white. In doing so, we can discover things about our partner we weren't even aware of. As long as the letter is written with love, respect, and sincerity, it's hard to imagine that it wouldn't be well received. And if you have no immediate concerns in which a letter might be helpful, congratulations. If this is the case, why not write a letter that simply says, "I love you"?

79.

DON'T MAKE YOUR PARTNER
WALK ON EGGSHELLS

When you ask around, as we have done, you'll find that there are many consistent comments that people make regarding what frustrates them in their relationships. Near the top of this "I wish things were different" list is the complaint, "I feel like I have to walk around on eggshells."

What a shame! You're in a relationship that is supposed to be mutually satisfying, and you're constantly worried that your partner is so used to sweating the small stuff that he or she is never more than seconds away from losing it, or from expressing some kind of disappointment, directed at you. You're constantly concerned that you might say or do something wrong, make a mistake, spill a glass of milk, or whatever else that will set your partner off.

As you read these paragraphs, ask yourself the question, "Are there ways that I encourage my partner to feel as though he or she must walk around on eggshells?" If you find yourself answering, "Yes," it may be time to reevaluate your priorities and perhaps even lower your expectations a little bit. If your partner seems to say "I'm sorry" a lot, or if he seems defensive a great deal of the time, it could indicate that he feels as though he must be cautious around you. If you're not sure whether or not you're contributing to this problem, it might be a good idea to ask your partner. Really! As difficult and humbling as it might be, it could be a huge step toward deepening your relationship and bringing the two of you closer together. A general rule of thumb is that most people are forgiving if they know you're working on your weaknesses. I remember asking Kris if she ever felt this way around me. To my surprise, she said that sometimes she did, particularly when clutter began to find its way into our home. She knows that too much clutter drives me nuts, and that sometimes she felt I was blaming her for our piles of mess. Since that time, I've been careful to pay attention when I'm frustrated by clutter, and to be sure I don't make her feel like it's her fault—which it isn't.

The good news is, once you realize that you're creating anxiety for your partner, it's probably going to be fairly easy to make some minor adjustments. Most people don't want to be bothered and irritated all the time, and most certainly don't want their loved ones to be frightened by their reactions. So, once your eyes are open to your habit, you can begin backing off when you're getting too uptight.

It's helpful to turn the tables. Can you imagine how difficult and stressful it would be if you felt insecure almost every time you opened your mouth, expressed an opinion or complaint, or completed a task? You'd be worried that you were going to say the wrong thing, or that you may not have cleaned the garage well enough, or prepared dinner just the right way, or that your partner was keeping score of your efforts. How much fun would that be? How long would you put up with it? The sad truth is, it's really difficult to be with someone when you feel as though you're constantly disappointing them. On the other hand, it's so nice and so easy to love someone when you feel like it's okay to be yourself, even when you make mistakes.

When someone feels as though they must walk around on eggshells, they almost always distance themselves from the person they are afraid of disappointing, thus creating a wedge in their relationship. Most people would much prefer feeling safe rather than constantly worried that they are doing something wrong. So they become more superficial and stop sharing whenever they feel they are at risk of undeserved criticism.

This is one of those hard-to-admit but easy-to-fix habits that occur in many relationships. The first step is to see that it's in everyone's best interest if no one has to feel as though they must walk around on eggshells. After that, the solution becomes paying attention to your own feelings of frustration. When you begin feeling tense, remind yourself to lighten up. Put things in perspective. Remind yourself that the quality of your relationship is infinitely more important than whatever it is that's bugging you. You'll find, when you do this, that your feelings of frustration will fade and your love of your partner will deepen.

80.

MAKE A PLAN TO BECOME
MORE LOVING

♥ It's extremely helpful to have a well-thought-out plan in place to ensure that you will become a more loving person. This is one of those instances where the intent of your plan is critical. We're not talking about creating a plan in order to get more love or to manipulate someone into loving you, but simply a plan designed to become the most loving person that you can become.

We always increase the odds of making something happen when we have a plan designed to take us where we want to go. For example, if we want to lose weight or become more physically fit, we create a diet or a fitness plan. In business, we create a business plan or a marketing plan or an advertising campaign—or we create sales goals. If we want to get through school, we map out a course plan. We decide which classes we need to take now so that we'll be able to take other classes later on down the road. It's almost always easier to get somewhere if you can master the steps along the way. Whenever you want to go from A to Z, it's almost always easier if you have a plan.

Becoming a more loving person is no exception to this rule. In other words, having a plan—short-term goals and long-term goals—and working toward those goals usually pays enormous dividends in terms of becoming the type of person you want to become.

We've met hundreds of people—in fact, almost everyone we meet falls into this category—who want more love in their lives. Most can identify what their ideal partner would be like or the ways they would like their existing partner to change. Surprisingly few, however, have a plan designed to help themselves become more loving. Yet, ironically, while you have little if any capacity to change someone else, you do have a great deal of influence over your own destiny.

When I first met Steve, he was a nice guy but, in his words, "more than a little uptight." He remembers being a somewhat poor listener, having a tendency to finish other people's sentences, and being heavily invested in being "right." He also described himself as being too reactive and tense, and almost always in a hurry. One of the things he had going for himself, however, was a sincere goal—and a long-term plan—to become a more loving human being. His plan included a commitment to becoming less stubborn and selfish while learning to be a more relaxed and grateful person.

He worked, daily, on his listening skills. He read books with differing points of view and practiced patience and gratitude. He took courses on communication and relationship skills, and he mastered several techniques on stress reduction, including yoga and meditation. These and other things helped him to make the changes he knew he wanted to make.

We watched him change, and over the years, he has become one of the most loving people we know. His presence is gentle and kind, and he has become one of the best and most patient listeners, as well as one of the most giving people, we've ever met. He is now happily married to a woman who is equally special. There's no question that his "plan"—knowing where he wanted to go and who he wanted to become—played a significant part in his success.

We all have the capacity to change and to become the people we want to be. Without a plan, however, it can be difficult or confusing to make sustainable changes. Having a plan in place can help us make those changes and bring them to life, whatever they happen to be, and makes our journey seem more manageable. Good luck.

81.

GRACEFULLY ACCEPT
APOLOGIES

♥ Sadly, many people find it difficult to apologize. Over the years, the two of us have heard a number of very wise people speculate that one of the reasons this might be true is because, when we do apologize, it's often accepted in a less than graceful manner. When this is the case, it takes some of the motivation away to continue apologizing, even when appropriate. This is a shame because most happy couples will insist that both offering and receiving apologies are integral parts of a loving and growing relationship.

I overheard what I thought was an excellent example of this problem while I was sitting at a coffee shop. With tears in her eyes, a woman was sharing with her husband that she was sorry that her work had become so consuming. Apparently, she had been traveling a great deal and was spending lots of time away from him and their children. I gathered that this was taking a toll on the family as well as on their relationship.

Obviously, I don't know all the facts, and they certainly aren't any of my business. However, regardless of the specifics, one thing was perfectly clear. His inability to soften and open his heart in response to her genuine and heartfelt apology was guaranteeing an escalation of any problems they were already having. Rather than hug her, hold her hand, or even reassure his wife, he gave her a disapproving look that seemed to make her heart sink.

While I have no way of knowing for sure, it appeared as though he was trying to make her feel even guiltier than she already did.

Like everyone who offers an apology, this woman was opening the door to loving communication, a possible compromise, or perhaps even a solution. In order for an apology to be effective, however, both parties must do their part. In this instance, the woman's husband wasn't willing to do so. Consequently, he was missing an opportunity to strengthen their relationship. He was increasing the likelihood that she would become less apologetic in the future, and that she might even begin to see him as the problem. When apologies aren't accepted, bitterness and resentment often creep into the picture.

Granted, most of us will probably not be quite as visibly ungraceful in our acceptance of an apology. However, we might push our partner away in other, more subtle ways. We might, for instance, mumble under our breath, sigh, make a condescending comment such as "It's about time," or in some other way minimize or fail to fully accept the apology.

We've found that, in most instances, an apology is an excellent opportunity to deepen our love and our partnership. It's an ideal time to make a genuine effort to listen deeply and respectfully. It's a time to experience empathy and gratitude for the fact that our partner is willing to apologize, which is something not everyone is able to do. Further, when we accept an apology, it makes it far more likely that our partner will do the same for us when it's our turn to apologize.

The next time your partner (or anyone else) offers an apology, see if you can really take it to heart. Soften your edges and open your heart. You may find that, despite whatever the apology is about, your relationship will be able to enter a new, even more rewarding, phase.

82.

REFLECT, FOR A MOMENT,
ON ALL YOU DON'T DO

This is a leveraged strategy for regaining perspective. It only takes a minute, but ideally, it should be done regularly. When taken seriously, it pays powerful and lasting dividends. Specifically, it addresses one of the most common "resentment traps" we have observed—the feeling that you do more than your partner; that nagging sense that your contribution is more significant or more consuming and that, somehow, it's not fair.

It's human nature to be focused on what you're doing. It's a way of keeping track of what is being done and what isn't. In a way, it's hard not to do this—your responsibilities are in your face, twenty-four hours a day. I don't think a day has gone by that I haven't heard someone (if not Kris or me) complain about having too much to do.

Sandra was often resentful of her husband Mike. She has three children and there's no question that she carries the bulk of the responsibility. She does a vast majority of the cooking, cleaning, laundry, help with the homework, driving to and from school, as well as the various activities the kids are involved with—sports, music, friends, and so forth. To be quite honest, it seems that she has a legitimate gripe. There's no question that her husband could be far more helpful around the home.

There is, however, another side of the story that was abruptly brought to her attention. Mike became quite ill and, for a while, it looked as if he might not recover.

Although Sandra had spent a great deal of time thinking about what she called the "unfair distribution of work," she had never taken the time to reflect on all that she doesn't do! Intellectually, of course, she had always known the same facts. What had happened, however, was that while her own contribution was with her, day in and day out, Mike's had become invisible. In the midst of her own busyness, there was no real need for Sandra to be thinking about the things she wasn't doing—they were being done for her.

In addition to working more than fifty hours a week outside the home and earning 100 percent of the family income, Mike was responsible for all of the yard work. He also was quite handy and fixed everything around the house. Since having their first child, Sandra had not worked outside the home, even for a single day. Nor had she mowed the lawn, clipped the hedge, or fixed a faucet. Mike had also been responsible for paying all the bills and keeping track of their finances. He was on top of their retirement planning, kept their financial records, and prepared their yearly taxes. These things, and many others, had become invisible to her.

It wasn't until the income ceased, the bills began piling up, the yard looked like a forest, and the dishwasher broke down that it suddenly hit her: How could she live without him? It became clear that there was so much she wasn't doing.

Please forgive our stereotypical example. Obviously this could be worded in many different ways. It's often the husband who needs to think of all *he* doesn't do. Also, it's obviously the case that the woman could be earning the household income while the man is home with the kids, or some combination of the two. The relevant fact is that, in almost all cases, regardless of how your life and responsibilities are divided up, it's both partners who need to reflect.

If you think about it, there are probably things you don't have to do, at least very often. Maybe you think there is an invisible housecleaner who whisks in to clean your home each day or a skilled short-order cook who sneaks in to prepare your meals. Perhaps the laundry or dishes are magically done on a regular basis, or the bills are paid, or the kids' lunches fixed, or the grocery shopping done, or other chores somehow just get handled. Or perhaps you haven't noticed that the garage is always organized, the car runs well, or that the kids somehow manage to have their hair cut on a regular basis, clothes and shoes that fit, and, on top of it all, that they almost always get to soccer practice on time. A man once said to me, in all seriousness, "We have four boys living in the house and it's amazing, but the toilets stay pretty clean." He didn't realize that his wife cleaned them every single day!

The idea isn't to compare who has it easier or tougher, nor is it about who's right and who's wrong. Instead, the idea is to spend a little less time thinking about all that you do—and a little more time reflecting on and appreciating all the things you don't have to do. If you can find even a single thing that you don't have to do—no matter how small it is—you will feel a hint of gratitude. You'll be amazed at how much resentment will fade away, how much less you'll be sweating the small stuff, and how much more you'll appreciate your partner by incorporating this exercise into your life.

83.

PRACTICE REGULAR STRESS PREVENTION

♥ There is a great deal that can be done, aside from dealing with your relationship, to help you become more relaxed and less reactive and to sweat the small stuff less often. Many of the most effective things you can do to become happier and more peaceful fall into a category that we like to call "stress prevention."

Stress prevention involves any activity or attitude that is designed (or tends) to produce, on its own, a calmer and more accepting attitude toward life. What's exciting and encouraging is that people who become more relaxed and peaceful—however they do it—are almost always able to bring that sense of peace into their relationships. They become more patient, kind, compassionate, and generous. In addition, they usually become better listeners and are able to take the ups and downs of relationships more in stride. Their behavior, in general, becomes more conducive to a loving relationship. They criticize less often, become less defensive and judgmental, dish out more compliments, become jealous less often, and are a lot easier to be around.

I once did an informal research study project that was designed to determine the effectiveness of various stress-reducing techniques. What I discovered was impressive but not surprising. It turned out that people who took a regular yoga or meditation class (once a week) were three times less likely to describe their relationships as being "stressful." And even when they did complain about their relationships, the complaints were usually minor and discussed with a sense of humor and perspective. There was a slightly less dramatic, yet similar statistic for people who exercised regularly and took care of themselves, who took time out to relax or to read inspiring books, or who took the time on a regular basis to pray, congregate with like-minded people, reflect, or study spiritual literature. It was obvious to me (and probably is to you as well) that taking some time each day, whenever possible, to attend to your inner self, and to cultivate a sense of well-being, however you do it, pays enormous dividends in your personal life and in your relationships. Remember, we're not talking about hours a day—more along the lines of thirty minutes or so.

Many people say, "I don't have time to read, or practice yoga, or meditate, or go to church, or sit still, or get a massage, or exercise, or whatever." Yet, when you get right down to it, if you want a loving relationship, it's actually the other way around: You don't have time NOT to do one or more of these kinds of things because when you do, the payoff is so substantial. And don't forget, the reverse is also true. People who don't do any of these things (or something else designed to ease stress and encourage perspective) are usually more tense, stubborn, and reactive, and can be difficult to be around.

We encourage you to explore, investigate, and try out your many stress-prevention options. There are stress-management courses in certain communities, people who offer massage and other forms of certified bodywork, dozens of different types of exercises, yoga and meditation classes, as well as many excellent books to read on these topics and others. I've heard of classes on optimism and other attitude-related perspectives, and I know that there are even a few classes on happiness itself, as I used to teach them myself.

I've found that I usually won't make the time to take a yoga class, but I have several really good videos that allow me to practice in the privacy and comfort of my home, at the time of my choice. Kris, in addition to other things, loves to go jogging, and does so almost every day. One of the things we love to do together is to meditate for a few minutes each morning. We don't make a really big deal out of any of these things. Yet, all of them, along with a positive mental outlook, help us to keep our stress levels under control and our sense of well-being fairly high. When you're happy and relaxed, life tends to appear pretty darn good. When this is the case, it's pretty difficult not to have an excellent relationship.

84.

DON'T SPEAK FOR YOUR SPOUSE (OR BOYFRIEND, GIRLFRIEND, FIANCÉE, OR ANYONE ELSE)!

"I hate it when she speaks for me." "I can't stand it when he puts words in my mouth." I can't tell you how often I've heard these and similar statements. Just last week, in fact, I was in the state of Wisconsin doing a speaking engagement. The evening before the event, I was attending a social gathering. At one point a man said to me, right in front of his wife, "She won't have any of those crackers. She doesn't like them." Less than a minute later, when he walked away, she said to me, "Would you mind handing me one of those crackers? I love them." When I hesitated for a split second, she said, "Oh, don't pay any attention to my husband. I hate it when he speaks for me—he does it all the time."

How sad. It was such a habit that she had learned to expect it. Although I couldn't quantify to what degree, it seemed obvious that this habit had driven a very destructive wedge between them. His need to speak for her had become such a "normal" part of their relationship that she had lost respect for him.

When you get right down to it, it's quite disrespectful to speak for someone else. Even if you mean no conscious harm, it certainly implies that you don't think your partner (or whomever else you're speaking for) is qualified to speak for themselves—you know them better than they do. You know what they want, what they're thinking, and what their decisions are going to be. They couldn't possibly change their mind or think differently this time. At any rate, if they did, you would be able to anticipate it! These disrespectful assumptions—combined with the fact that it's one of the things a vast majority of adults can't stand—make speaking for someone else an excellent candidate to put on your "Try never to do this again" list.

This is one of those habits that can sneak up on you every once in a while. When you know someone really well, it's easy to assume that you really do know what they're thinking or what their wishes will be. And you might be right most of the time. But, despite your excellent odds of making a correct assumption, it's still not worth it.

I think both Kris and I do a pretty good job of avoiding this tendency. If we do slip up, at least we know it wasn't in anyone's best interest. Both of us do find ourselves speaking for our children, however, so we're still working on that one.

If you find yourself speaking for someone else, be easy on yourself. Rather than making a big deal out of it, gently remind yourself that it's almost never a good idea. And if someone you love is doing it to you—well, try not to sweat it too much! On the other hand, when the timing is right, you might want to gently remind your significant other that, while you certainly appreciate the thought, you're quite capable of speaking for yourself!

85.

CONSPIRE TO INSPIRE

One of the decisions we're both very happy about is that, early on in our relationship, we made the decision to "conspire to inspire." We decided that we would like to be mutual sources of inspiration for one another, personally, professionally, and every other way.

When you conspire to inspire, you do a lot more than act as a cheerleader for your partner's efforts. Your motivation is to help your partner become all that he or she can be—not necessarily what *you* want them to be, but rather you help them fulfill their own dreams and desires by believing in them, encouraging them, and sticking beside them in good times and bad. It means that, even though you may not completely understand certain decisions your partner is making, you give them the benefit of the doubt, whenever possible. You assume the best. Rather than criticizing or questioning, you seek first to understand and to be supportive.

Kris has always been a source of inspiration to me. She has always believed in me, even during those times when I doubted myself. When I was in college, for example, I was a top-ranked tennis player. I knew, however, that I was ready to quit and pursue what I felt were less self-oriented goals. I wanted to become involved in the helping fields; I wanted to join the Big Brothers of America program and refocus my entire life. I wanted to learn more about psychology and happiness.

Virtually everyone—my friends, teammates, tennis coach—gave me a difficult time, except Kris. Some even laughed at me. Many thought I was a candidate for tennis pro, and no one, other than Kris and my family, could understand why I would give up a sport I had worked so hard at—one that could earn someone good enough a great deal of money and fame.

But from the time we had first met, we had conspired to inspire. She knew my heart wasn't in tennis anymore—it was elsewhere. She encouraged me in every way she knew how to trust my instincts, follow my bliss, and "go for it." In fact, she came right out and said it: "Richard, I think you should quit."

Other girls I knew quickly lost interest in me—I was no longer an athlete on campus. It became instantly obvious that Kris loved me for who I was and what I wanted to become, instead of who she wanted me to be or who she wanted me to become. Shortly after this experience, we fell in love—for good.

She repeated this process early on in my career. I had a small business, but really wanted to write full time. Despite giving up any financial security we had, she not only encouraged me to follow my dream, she insisted. She reminded me, "It's my job to help inspire you. You know what you want to do—go for it."

What I've learned is that couples who stick together with love and ongoing respect conspire to inspire each other in their own unique ways. Individuals who freely speak of their partner in loving ways often use the words, "My partner is a source of inspiration."

It's never too late to start. All you have to do is make the decision to become a greater source of inspiration. If you're unclear about how to do this, ask your partner! Ask the question, "What could I do—or how could I act—that would make me a greater source of support?" This may end up being one of the most important questions you ever ponder. Give this strategy a try. It will inspire both of you.

86.

CAST AWAY JEALOUSY

(KRIS)

Love is not jealous. Period. In fact, there is almost nothing that can suffocate a good feeling between two people faster, or with more certainty, than jealousy. It is, however, one of the easiest human emotions to understand. Jealousy stems from insecurity, and insecurity comes from feelings and thoughts of inadequacy. One of the only ways a person can create feelings of inadequacy is to first compare himself or herself to others.

There seem to be two essential ingredients that will help you cast jealousy out of your life. First and foremost, it's important to accept the fact that there is always going to be someone out there who has something you do not—more money, better looks, greater charisma, a longer list of achievements, or whatever. So what? Good for them. Stop comparing yourself to others and you'll be amazed at how much better you'll feel about yourself. Remember, you have also been gifted with unique talents and attributes that others don't enjoy. Spend your mental energy focusing on these gifts, and be grateful for your own ability to make a contribution.

Second, in your relationships, try to embrace the idea that one person will not fill all of your needs, nor will you fill all of theirs. And that's okay. This is hard for many people to accept, as it brings up feelings of inadequacy. It's a nice fantasy to think of yourself as being on an island with the one perfect person of your dreams, but we don't live that way and neither were we meant to.

We are here to share our life energy with others; to grow and be nurtured, to nurture and grow. Sometimes that means having relationships and friendships of the opposite sex even though we are committed to our partner. I am, of course, speaking of *platonic* friendship. Allowing your partner to choose his or her friendships based not on gender, but on preference, is one of the greatest gifts you can give. By doing so, you are, in effect, acknowledging that you don't own your partner; you are merely fortunate to be chosen as the most special person in his or her life to spend time with. With your actions, you show a trust so deep it reaches to the heart of your commitment as a couple.

Recently, I made plans to have coffee with an old friend who happens to be a boyfriend from long ago. It had been ten years since I had seen him, and for whatever reason, it felt very important to me to reconnect with him. I felt perfectly comfortable sharing this with Richard, knowing that, without a doubt, he trusts me completely and would not feel insecure in any way. Richard's first priority in our relationship has always been my happiness. He isn't concerned about what form that happens to take. He confirmed his feelings of trust by not questioning me or feeling insecure; instead, he encouraged me to go and have fun, as I knew he would. I have always marveled at his personal stability and have tried to mirror that same feeling of trust.

We both have many friendships. Some are together, as a couple, and some are separate. All of these relationships help to round out our lives and fulfill us in different ways. I would be crazy to think that I could be all things to Richard. To deny him his chosen friendships, male or female, would seem selfish, insecure, and cruel.

Most of us have witnessed firsthand how jealousy has smothered a relationship. When you find yourself feeling insecure or having feelings of inadequacy, try to gently reflect on your thoughts. See if you are busy comparing yourself to others. Are you making up stories that exist only in your mind? Tell yourself that it's okay that you cannot fill all of your partner's needs, and remind yourself how and why your partner chose you as that special person to share his life with. If you can cast away jealousy, you will experience a freedom from insecurity that will nurture your relationship forever.

87.

ALLOW YOUR PARTNER
A FEW ECCENTRICITIES

In a fun, innocent sort of way, our eccentricities help to define us. They outline our preferences and define us as unique and different from others.

For example, I would say that a few of my eccentricities are (1) a strong preference for a lack of clutter and (2) a weird, almost total inability to be late. I love open space, lacking in piles of paper and other stuff. For whatever reason, clutter makes me uncomfortable. On the other hand, open space makes me feel peaceful.

I also love to allow myself plenty of time so that I'm not in a constant hurry. I associate rushing around with stress and frustration, while I associate a lack of hurry with peace and serenity. These simple preferences bring me an enormous amount of joy.

One of the easiest and, I believe, most charming characteristics of Kris is her willingness to allow me to have these and other eccentricities without mocking or hassling me. Rather than give me a hard time, question my motives, criticize or judge me, she just allows me to be me. In other words, she doesn't "sweat it." It's perfectly okay with her that these things are important to me. She's well aware that I can go overboard with these preferences, and I'm sure that, at times, they can be a little annoying. Obviously, with two children and lots going on in our family, it's not always possible to have a lack of clutter, nor is it always possible to be on time.

The point, however, is that she makes allowances for my preferences even though she's not as invested as I am in these particular areas. This doesn't mean she always accommodates me, but in a respectful way, she humors me and goes along with my eccentricities, whenever she can. Rather than wishing I would do things differently, she sees me as a "character." For example, we have a few areas in the house where it's almost never cluttered. If these areas begin to pile up, she's likely to put the piles somewhere else. Also, when I'm making a big deal out of getting somewhere on time, she plays along, not because it's an emergency, but because she loves me—and she knows it makes me happy to be on time. Several times, for example, when we were running late to an appointment, she has suggested in a loving tone, "Why don't you drive your own car and I'll meet you in a little while?" I can think of many instances where it would have been easy for her to give me a lecture or criticize me in some way, but she didn't. Compare that response to yelling out in a harsh tone, "Don't worry about it, I'll be ready in a minute. Stop being so obsessed!"

People have all sorts of different eccentricities. Some people are a little obsessed with being clean. Others like to eat a certain food on a specific day. Some insist on putting things in a certain place, spending a certain amount of time alone, being organized, washing a dish as soon as it's used, going to sleep at a certain time, reading at a certain time, spending Thursday night with the girls (or guys), or whatever. There are probably millions of examples.

One of the simple pleasures of life is feeling the freedom to be yourself and to do some things just the way you like to do them, without having to qualify your reasons or constantly explain yourself—as long as they aren't adversely affecting others. When you have the need to correct your partner, make him "wrong" or feel bad, or criticize his eccentricities, you rob him of a simple source of joy.

We're not suggesting you buy into, encourage, or condone truly neurotic behavior—or anything that is disruptive or damaging. Instead, we are referring to innocent little daily preferences that, for whatever reason, bring you (or your partner) joy. We're suggesting that when you allow your partner a few eccentricities, even if they conflict with the way you might do something, you'll be nourishing an important need of the human heart—the need to be oneself.

88.

STOP BEING SO DEMANDING

❤️ Pause for a moment and reflect on how it feels when someone acts demanding toward you. What's it like when they are impatient, bossy, and picky? How does it feel when someone is looking over your shoulder making sure you're doing your part and living up to their expectations? The answer to these questions can be summarized in a single word—Yuck!

Generally speaking, people resist and often resent people who are unreasonably demanding, particularly when they are in what is supposed to be a loving relationship. Invariably, the partner on the receiving end of the demands will ask herself the question, "What right does he have to treat me like that?" The way we see it, it's an excellent question.

Most people seem to feel that being demanding is a distasteful human quality. People who are too demanding are seen as difficult, selfish, self-righteous, and judgmental. They might be described as people who sweat the small stuff whenever they can't get others to do what they want. Demanding people are hard to be around and, unfortunately, difficult to love. When you are around a demanding person, you may feel a sense of pressure, always wondering whether you're measuring up. People who live with demanding partners often describe their experience as "having to walk around on eggshells," or as constantly being on guard.

Someone we know was married to one of the most demanding people we've ever met. His demands ranged from his insistence that she not spend time with her girlfriends, to the amount of time she was able to spend at work. He demanded that she be accountable for every cent she spent, and that she be able to justify her phone bill. He monitored her diet and insisted she read certain books. It became so obnoxious that she left him.

Fortunately, most people aren't nearly as demanding. Yet, it's easy to become demanding in far more subtle ways. We might, for example, demand to know where our partner was during every moment of the day. Or we might demand that the house look a certain way and, when it doesn't, we sulk or complain. Perhaps we demand that our partner share certain beliefs or preferences. Or we demand that they participate in hobbies, gatherings, or activities that they aren't as interested in as we are. There are many ways that a demanding personality presents itself.

We often associate a demanding personality with someone who is loud and bossy. But demanding people aren't always this way. Sometimes they are quiet and sulky. Other times they are "passive aggressive," meaning they will attempt to avoid appearing demanding but their aggression will come out in subtle ways when their demands aren't being met.

Keep in mind that being around a demanding person is very stressful and no fun at all. It might be a good idea to consider the ways that you might be acting a little demanding. If and when you identify what they are, make a gentle effort to back off. In all likelihood, you'll be rewarded with a much less stressed-out partner who is easier and more fun to be with.

89.

WHEN IN DOUBT, PAUSE

♥ This strategy might appropriately be called an "irritation stopper." Over the years it has helped the two of us, individually and as a couple, to keep our irritation, annoyance, and frustration with one another to an absolute minimum. It addresses the inevitable problem of overreacting to some little thing your partner says or does. It keeps you from turning day-to-day "small stuff" into big stuff.

So often, in retrospect, it's easy to look back and realize that something that upset us at the moment wasn't really that big a deal after all. It just seemed like it was. One of the reasons so many things seem so urgent is that, rather than pausing to reflect, we react instantly to our initial impulse. Our mind latches onto a thought and we allow ourselves to get carried away.

Robert serves as an excellent example. For the most part, he's a tremendously nice person who is generous and thoughtful. The one thing that his girlfriend, Stephanie, was having trouble with was his tendency to overreact and assume the worst. When confronted with a potential hassle or problem, he could, in a matter of seconds, blow it out of proportion and turn it into a really big deal.

For example, on one occasion Stephanie said to Robert, "My parents are coming into town and I told them we could spend some time with them."

Immediately, Robert flew into a panic and started reminding her of how busy he was and how he had told her he didn't have any time the next few weeks. His mind created an emergency. He pictured the four of them spending day after day together, engaged in small talk, while his priorities were put on the back burner. He accused her of not respecting his time or his wishes.

Robert hadn't given Stephanie enough time to explain that her parents were only coming in for the evening, as they had a three-hour layover at the airport. Her parents lived on the other side of the country and she thought it would be a great (and rare) chance for the four of them to spend a few hours together. That's it; no other expectations whatsoever. It truly wasn't a big deal.

As is so often the case, Robert became embarrassed by his overreaction and then had to spend a great deal of time apologizing for his conduct. He realized that his girlfriend wasn't involved in a conspiracy to take over his schedule—she simply wanted to share him with her parents. Sometimes it's awesome to think about how much time and energy you could save, and how much nicer your relationship could be, if you could eliminate or even reduce these and thousands of other, similar types of reactions. In most instances, all that it takes is a reflective pause. The rest takes care of itself.

It won't always be the case, but most of the time, if you take a moment to pause before reacting, it will allow you to gather your bearings as well as your perspective. Even if something still seems important, it probably won't seem quite so urgent. There's something in the pause itself that creates a sense of peace and allows your wisdom to surface. There's no question that pausing will help you avoid sweating the small stuff. And in doing so, it will nourish your relationship.

90.

PRACTICE
UNCONDITIONAL LOVE

Many spiritual philosophies advocate the practice of unconditional love. And why not? Unconditional love is, perhaps, the ultimate expression of love. It says, "I love you because you are you. You don't have to be any different from who you are to receive and secure my love." There are no conditions attached to the love. You don't have to lose weight, make a certain amount of money, agree with everything I say, behave according to my plans, share all of my goals, or smile at me when you don't want to. It's even okay when you're insecure or depressed, or when you make mistakes—I love you anyway. You don't have to be perfect, or even close to it.

Other than our own children (and only then when they are very tiny), it's probable that few of us (if any) will ever love someone entirely unconditionally. Whether we know it or not, we usually place certain conditions on our love and we have a number of expectations (e.g., you must behave in certain ways to secure my love—you must put me first, you must be faithful, you must not have friends, or express fondness toward members of the opposite sex, you must think like me, prioritize my goals, and so forth).

Yet, as with other worthwhile endeavors where perfection is nearly impossible—health, fitness, financial security, being really organized, to name just a few—it's still an excellent idea to point yourself in that direction, to have really high ideals, realizing that there are certain limitations on how well you are going to be able to do. For example, even though you probably will never be perfectly healthy (whatever that means), it's nevertheless important to make good diet, exercise, and lifestyle choices if you want to be as healthy as possible. Likewise, although you may never be completely organized, you'll be far more so if you implement some proven strategies such as using files, simplifying, and regularly getting rid of things you no longer need or use. The more committed you are to being totally organized, the more organized you will end up being. I once had the goal of running a three-hour marathon. While, unfortunately, I fell nine seconds short of my goal, there's no question that I came far closer to reaching that goal than I would have had my goal been to run a four-hour marathon.

So it is with unconditional love. Despite the fact that we're probably doomed to never reach perfection, we can certainly come much closer to reaching our goal of unconditional love if we set lofty goals. For example, we can "catch ourselves" when we become judgmental or behave in unkind ways. We can strive to become less jealous and demanding and replace those tendencies with gratitude and softness. Or we can become better listeners and more forgiving. We can commit to being the first person to act loving— even when our partner can't or won't do so. We can also begin to make allowances for the fact that our partner will, at times, fall into low moods and will say and do things that aren't to our liking—and we can choose to love them in those moments just the same as when they are feeling loving and acting kindly toward us.

There are literally hundreds of other things we can do to become more unconditionally loving—everything from taking a class on effective communication or listening skills; to asking your partner what changes he or she would like to see in you, if they could wave a magic wand; to reading spiritual and inspiring material designed to help you become more unconditionally loving. In fact, you can almost turn it into a game—making it a personal challenge to see how well you can do.

While there are no specific ground rules to follow, there is a consistent result that you can count on, and that is this: You can be sure that whatever efforts you make in order to become a more unconditionally loving partner, you will see results in the quality of your relationship. This is one of those strategies where you have absolutely nothing to lose—and everything to gain.

91.

GO AHEAD AND DO IT

With the dozens of daily responsibilities that most of us are expected or required to do, it's inevitable that at least a few things are going to slip through the cracks—you'll leave some laundry on the floor or a few dishes in the sink. Perhaps a bill needing to be paid will be overlooked, you forget to pick up the rental movie you promised you would, or you won't have time to make the bed. Or whatever.

One of the ways we create problems and ill feelings in our relationships is by silently (or, worse yet, vocally) demanding that our partner never slip up. We say or think things like, "You forgot to do the dishes" or "You put the towels in the wrong bathroom," as if our partner is a robot needing reprogramming. In reality, of course, the person you love isn't a robot, but simply a person, just like you, who innocently forgot, or was too tired or too preoccupied to take care of it. What's the big deal?

Usually, a more effective, less abrasive, and often even less energy-draining way to relate to your partner's slip-ups is to simply go ahead and do it yourself—not with any resentment or regret, or by turning it into a scene—but rather quietly, selflessly, and lovingly. In other words, if the dishes in the sink are bothering you, go ahead and wash them. Or, if your partner somehow neglected to pay a bill that needs to be paid, go ahead and pay it instead of reminding him how forgetful he can be. These and so many other things are the epitome of "small stuff." What's nice is that, in the absence of these negative distractions, you're left with more energy to focus on the truly important aspects of your relationship—good communication, sharing, laughing, loving, spiritual growth, and all the rest.

Inevitably, when we discuss this issue in public, someone will stand up and say, "Hey, wait a minute. If I took that lenient approach, my partner would never do another dish or pay another bill. I'd be stuck doing everything." And to a minuscule percentage of the population this may be true. Frankly, however, it's not very likely. To the contrary, if you can avoid lecturing your partner, snapping, yelling, reacting, and any other tendencies to become adversarial, you may be amazed at how helpful your partner will become. The key is timing. It's best to discuss any issues and concerns you might be having about fairness, forgetfulness, or chores when you're both in a nondefensive, loving mood, instead of when you're fuming about the socks on the floor.

We're not asking you to roll over and allow yourself to be taken advantage of. Rather, it's a matter of recognizing that, for most of us, life is complicated, chaotic, and demanding. Very few people feel they have enough time, and almost everyone feels that they have too much to do. Therefore, often our only emotional sanctuary or environment where we can let our guards down is when we are with our partner. So, when that's taken away, or no longer true—when we feel that even our partner is keeping track of how we're doing and not making allowances for the fact that we're human—it leads to disillusionment and frustration.

So while you probably *don't* want to take on even more than you're already doing, when something needs to be done (even when it's not technically your responsibility), often the best solution is to go ahead and do it. In most instances, when you make this decision, you'll find greater harmony in your relationship. This has certainly been our experience.

92.

SAY THE WORDS,
"I'M SORRY"

I asked an acquaintance of mine a very direct question. It was, "How often does your husband say the words, 'I'm sorry?'" Her answer explains the necessity of including this strategy in this book. Her answer was, "You're kidding, right?"

It turns out that he never apologizes. She claimed that this is true, even when it's obvious that he made a mistake, caused her grief, or said something mean, insensitive, or condescending. This was a bit surprising because, on the surface, her husband seems like a really nice person.

I wondered if their situation was unique, so I began asking around. All in all, I must have talked to hundreds of people from all over the country. Much to my surprise, not all but most of the people I asked also reported that the words "I'm sorry" were a minimal, if not practically nonexistent part of their relationship. What's more, it turned out that even those who say the words "I'm sorry" often do so under their breath or mumbling, lacking a genuine sincerity.

I'm not sure why this is the case. It could be too much pride, a hardened ego, a lack of reflection, an inability to see oneself as part or all of a problem, or some combination of these things. Whatever the reason, I do know it's a mistake. Saying you're sorry, when appropriate, is an extremely healing and nurturing thing to do. It's seen by the recipient not as a sign of weakness, but of strength. It clears the air and opens the door to forgiveness and a fresh start. It brings trust, integrity, and humility into a relationship, three of the most beautiful qualities two people can share.

Luckily, we haven't had too many earth-shattering things to apologize to one another for. However, there have been times when Kris deserved a genuine apology and explanation for something I had done. Yet, even when the circumstances might have warranted a more insecure reaction, the apology proved to be the catalyst for enormous growth in our relationship, allowing us to talk about even painful things.

And we're not unique. It's extremely eye-opening to talk to couples who report that their partner does, in fact, use the words "I'm sorry" freely, when appropriate. They will tell you that, in many instances, the "mistake" that preceded the need for an apology was worth it, if for no other reason than the apology almost always brought them closer together as a couple. For example, Deborah had been overspending on her credit cards for years, which had created a multitude of financial problems. Her husband, Dan, had become quietly resentful. Each time they tried to discuss it, Deborah would either become defensive or, at best, she would claim she would "work on it."

I asked her if she was aware of the pain and fear she was causing Dan. She said that she was, but that she didn't know what to do about it. When I suggested she sit down with Dan and offer him a sincere, heartfelt apology, she became visibly uncomfortable. After a few moments, she said with a tear in her eye that she had been too ashamed and afraid to do so, but that she would try.

When I saw Dan again, he was happier than I had ever seen him. It turned out that he was more resentful of her lack of apology than he was of her spending habits. He said that her willingness to say she was sorry opened the door to deeper and less defensive communication, including their joint decision to visit a therapist.

Whether it's over major things or everyday minor things, saying the words "I'm sorry" will usually work to your advantage. It's one of those ever-so-important phrases to introduce to your relationship.

93.

STAY AWAY
FROM COMPARISONS

♥ Shortly after our first child was born, we were at a friend's house having dinner with a small group of people. At some point during the evening our friend Cassie said to several others, "I wish David (her husband) would spend more time with our children like Richard does." Her husband overheard the comment and was furious. He interpreted her words to mean that she felt that I loved and prioritized my child more than he loved his, which was not only ridiculous, but would predictably anger most parents as well. Sadly, that was the beginning of the end of that friendship.

As is almost always the case, the comparison was ludicrous and unfair, like apples and oranges. I was self-employed and had a great deal of control over my schedule. I also worked less than fifteen minutes from home. David, on the other hand, worked for a giant company and had very little control over his schedule—if he wanted to keep his job. To make matters worse, his commute was well over an hour each way.

I'm certain that, in reality, our friend meant no harm by her comment. She was merely expressing her frustration that David couldn't spend more time with the kids. She also thought it was nice that I not only could make the time, but chose to spend lots of time with our child.

Unfortunately, however, all of that innocent, accurate, and legitimate explanation was, and usually is, meaningless. Once you compare someone who loves you to someone else, you've opened the door for potential trouble. If you think about it, it makes sense. Most of us want to be loved for who we are. It's a bit insulting to think that our partner wishes we were more like someone else. Hopefully, comparing your partner to someone else isn't going to make or break your relationship. Yet, it's one of those actions that has little, if any, upside.

There is another side of the coin to be aware of as well. If you're on the receiving end of a comparison, try not to "sweat it." Instead, try to see the innocence in your partner and let it go. Realize that, in most cases, when your partner compares you to someone else, they are merely expressing a temporary dissatisfaction in their own life. In Cassie's case, she was longing for her husband to have more free time with the kids. She knew it wasn't his fault. Had David seen the innocence in her comments, his reaction probably would have been much softer and more reflective. In fact, seen from a certain perspective, it could have led the two of them to some very deep and important communication about their priorities as a family.

We believe this strategy is a good one to tuck away on your permanent "back burner" of good ideas. We've yet to meet someone who appreciates being compared (in a deficient sort of way) to someone else. Nor do we expect to any time soon. Comparisons are indeed something we should all stay away from.

94.

LEARN FROM A TEEN

♥ Yipes! Absurd. Never! These are some of the first thoughts that might come to mind with the mere mention of learning from a teen (or an even younger person). How could a teen possibly teach us something about love?

It's an interesting exercise to think back to the first time you fell in love. Your parents and other adults probably labeled it "puppy love." Your feelings were most likely minimized or even dismissed. But think for a moment about those feelings and, when you do, be as honest as you can with yourself.

Wasn't it true that when you first fell in love, you could spend virtually every moment of the day with that special person—and never feel bored or preoccupied? Then, the moment you got home, you probably couldn't wait to talk to him or her on the phone. When you couldn't be together, you were thinking of each other. You could, as the cliché suggests, "gaze into each other's eyes." Hours apart felt like an eternity. Your every thought surrounded that person.

To your parents, of course, that wasn't "real love." No way. Theirs was the real thing! Sure, they may have bickered most of the time. More than likely they never expressed the slightest affection for one another and, in fact, didn't even appear to even like each other much of the time. They argued frequently and appeared to avoid spending time together. Far from gazing into each other's eyes, they rarely made eye contact. But, despite these facts, their relationship was defined as a "love relationship," whereas yours was a passing fancy.

Obviously, there are usually legitimate differences between the typical "first love" and a mature, committed relationship—hormones, age, time spent together, familiarity, level of responsibility, to name just a few. And we're not minimizing the effects of these factors. Nevertheless, there are at least a few key relationship boosters that can serve us grownups well. Two, in particular, stand out.

Attentiveness is a quality that seems to disappear over time. It's interesting to watch how attentive youngsters can be in their relationships. Recently, I saw two young people in love sitting together on a park bench. It was a windy day and some hair had blown into the young girl's eye. The young man gently reached over and pulled the hair out of her eye, which brought forth a beautiful smile of gratitude. Just then, the wind blew her folder off the bench, scattering papers all around. Immediately, without even thinking, he jumped up, gathered the papers for her, and returned to his seat. Just watching them made me smile. In fact, it reminded me that I hadn't brought Kris flowers for quite a while, and I decided to do so that evening.

On the bench directly across from the young couple was a more serious-looking duo. Because of the way they were acting and the rings on their fingers, I'm assuming they were married. It was a little funny to witness their reactions to the same wind. Whereas to the young couple, the wind was a chance to be attentive and to do nice things for one another, to the married couple, it was nothing but a source of irritation. Similar opportunities to be attentive presented themselves but were never acted on. In a word, they were grouchy. It was one of those sad scenes that could send a negative message about marriage and commitment.

The other consistent quality we have observed about teens in love is enthusiasm. It's almost magical to observe the zest and aliveness that many young people bring to a relationship. When we talk to our teenage babysitters about their boyfriends, it's fun to hear them describe how wonderful and exciting everything is. A phone call or simple note is seen as a gift. In comparison, when you listen to conversations in the men's locker room at the health club, you'd get the impression marriage was boring, habitual, and lifeless. I've yet to listen to one man discuss his wife in a truly enthusiastic, upbeat manner. Several times, I've left with a feeling of sadness.

It's interesting to consider how contagious enthusiasm can be to a relationship. In other words, when you speak, think, and act enthusiastically, you'll usually notice a corresponding reaction from your partner. When you're happy, upbeat, and enthused about life, it will rub off. On the other hand, when you're heavy-hearted and serious, and when you lack genuine enthusiasm, you'll encourage those types of feelings from your partner, as well.

It's just something to think about! So, if you can get beyond the logical explanations of why adult, "committed" relationships must be so different from those of young teens, you might actually learn something. The two of us certainly have—and there isn't a day that goes by that we aren't grateful for these insights.

95.

STEP ASIDE FROM STUBBORNNESS

This past weekend one of our daughter's friends spent the weekend with us. Watching two children play and interact has always been especially rewarding for us. About halfway through the weekend, however, the two of them had a huge argument about some game they were playing. Their fun and laughter came to an abrupt halt. Because each of them was acting particularly stubborn, and each was demanding an apology from the other, the argument ended up disrupting and interfering with a huge portion of their day.

Although a part of us was smiling because, in truth, it was really cute, we nevertheless couldn't help but reflect on the destructive power of stubbornness; how being stubborn squelches our fun and interferes with the qualities of a nurturing and satisfying relationship.

It's easy to see how an example like this applies to grownup relationships as well. Stubbornness has the potential to invade even the best of relationships. It's one of those qualities that consistently shows up as an answer to the question, "If you could change one thing about your partner, what would it be?" Indeed, very few people find stubbornness to be an endearing or nurturing quality.

It has always seemed to us that disagreements, failure to see eye to eye, and at least some conflict is inevitable. How could two people who live together, or who are in any type of deep or intimate relationship, possibly avoid at least some strife or conflict? Don't we all tend to see things a little differently, at least some of the time? And isn't it true that we are sometimes so convinced that we are "right" that we can even use other people's arguments to prove our positions? That's because we all see things our own way and we usually feel we're seeing things correctly, even when we're not.

Looking back on our daughter's weekend, it's obvious that the problem wasn't really the argument, but the corresponding stubbornness. Had either girl simply said, "Oh let's forget about it. I'm really sorry. Can we just start over?" there would have been a different outcome. The whole thing, regardless of what it was about, who started it, or whose fault it was, would have left like a passing storm, over in a matter of seconds.

It's the same with the rest of us. It's easy to blame our partner, or an issue, or an argument, fight, or disagreement for our unhappiness. The truth is, however, that most of the time the real culprit is our own stubbornness—our unwillingness to let go of something, to admit we were wrong or partially to blame, or to give up the need to be "right." If we can drop our defenses, tame our ego, and let go of our need to be so stubborn, it's remarkable how quickly most issues will resolve themselves, painlessly and without too much effort. The key seems be a steadfast belief that stubbornness, not our partner, is the enemy. Success lies not in righteousness, but in humility.

In a way, stubbornness is the antithesis of being lighthearted. In fact, if your goal was to take yourself even more seriously, a good place to start would be to become even more stubborn. There seems to be a direct relationship between lesser stubbornness and higher-quality relationships. So we hope you'll give this strategy some thoughtful consideration and some ongoing effort. We think you'll agree that stepping aside from stubbornness is a goal worth striving toward.

96.

RAISE YOUR STANDARD
OF LIVING

♥ We couldn't resist including this strategy in our book because, on the surface, it appears to contradict much of what I've written about in the past! However, rest assured, I'm not referring to raising your material standard of living, but rather the manner in which you live.

One of our favorite quotes, from an unknown source, says it this way: "What you do speaks so loud that I can't hear what you say." We interpret this to mean that our lives really are our greatest message. The way we live—our integrity, honesty, humility, sense of well-being, compassion, generosity, willingness to forgive, and various other noble qualities—demonstrates, above all, the kind of person we really are.

The implications of raising the manner in which we live for our personal relationships is profound. As we raise our standards for ourselves, others will feel and may even be touched by the changes in our lives. In other words, as we become less selfish and greedy, others will be drawn to us. As we become kinder, softer, and perhaps a better listener, those whom we meet will relax around us and will want to share themselves with us. Our ability to become more humble and gentle will be noticed, or at least sensed, by all who know us.

I met Bruce shortly after his thirty-fifth birthday. When I first met him, he complained of an inability to maintain a healthy relationship. Externally, he had it all. He was good looking and had a nice manner. He appeared healthy and had a dynamite career. He had many interesting hobbies and plenty of money to enjoy them. Furthermore, he was friendly and had a pretty good sense of humor.

So what's the catch?

After talking to him for less than an hour, it became clear that Bruce was a little on the self-absorbed side. He loved to talk about himself, but rarely asked questions about others. He enjoyed talking, but wasn't a very good listener. His mind would wander and he would appear disinterested until it was his turn to talk again. It wasn't hard to see why someone like Bruce, despite many nice qualities, might find it difficult to be in a quality, long-term relationship.

The good news was that Bruce had enough humility and wisdom to know something wasn't quite right and that he needed some help. He went to a counselor who convinced him that, while he did have many fine qualities, he needed a little work on his human and spiritual skills. Specifically, the counselor's goal was to teach him about the joys of listening and of getting to know others on an intimate level.

Quite by chance, I saw him briefly a few years later and was immediately struck by the changes in him. He told me that over a period of time, he had gone through a major transition. His newfound interest in others and his improved listening skills seemed to have transformed him into a much more generous, wise, and interesting person. You could feel a different kind of presence. He was calmer and more at ease with people. He seemed happier. I was delighted to hear that he was engaged to be married. It was easy to see why—he had raised his standard of living.

For Bruce, raising his standard of living centered around becoming less self-absorbed. For others, it might involve becoming less defensive or perhaps a little more forgiving. There are many ways I'm trying to raise my own standard of living—I'm trying to become more patient, less inclined to interrupt others, and less hyper, to name just three.

There's no question that raising your standard of living—whatever that means for you—will reap huge dividends in the quality of your relationships. You'll see instant results with each positive change you implement. The sky's the limit on this one—all of us have things to work on.

97.

ALLOW YOUR PARTNER THE SPACE TO "LOSE IT" EVERY ONCE IN A WHILE

It doesn't matter who you are or how little you "sweat it," there are probably going to be times when life just plain gets to you. There is something so refreshing and freeing about being with someone who allows you the space to "lose it" every once in a while—without judging you, correcting you, lecturing you, or trying to talk you out of it. It seems that when you're in the presence of someone who doesn't freak out when you freak out, there is often a calming transference that takes place. It helps you relax, regain your perspective, and get over whatever it was you were so upset about.

I don't seem to lose it very often. I'm lucky in that. Not always, but most of the time, I'm happy and content. One of the nice perks about being in a relationship with Kris, however, is that when I do lose it, it has little, if any, effect on her. Rather than becoming reactive, she remains compassionate and just takes it in stride. I remember asking her once, "Why doesn't it upset you when I fall apart?" Her answer has always stuck with me and, in fact, has helped me to keep my perspective and sense of humor during many such "emotional tests." She said, "I don't see any reason why you should be exempt from the rest of us." What she was getting at, of course, was that we're all in essentially the same boat. We're all doing the best that we can, but the truth is, all of us have unique problems, troubles, pressures, issues, fears, and concerns. So what else is new? Sometimes when I'm really frustrated and wishing my troubles would disappear, I ask myself the same question: "Richard, why should you be exempt from the rest of us?" Try it sometime—it really puts things into perspective.

The next time your partner "loses it" over something that's truly not an emergency, try this experiment. Rather than becoming upset or overly concerned about your partner's frustration, just stay calm. Be compassionate, yet don't react. Allow them to vent, yell, complain, or anything else (within reason) that they seem to need to do.

You might be pleasantly surprised at the result. In many instances, your partner may sense your peace of mind and begin to relax. Often, when people express their frustration, there is a sense that it's not okay to do so. If you can remain relatively unaffected, your partner may feel a sense of relief they have never felt before, a sense that they were listened to without judgment and that they were given the space to be human. It's strange because you don't have to *do* anything—except be there for your partner. In fact, it's more a matter of what you *don't* do that's ultimately so powerful.

In a strange way, I think I lose it less often simply because I know in my heart that it would be okay if I did. I imagine that if I felt insecure about expressing my feelings around Kris, it would create additional pressure to deal with.

So, we hope you'll experiment with this idea. It's very comforting to be around someone who allows you to "lose it" every once in a while. The act of remaining calm will almost always bring the two of you even closer together.

98.

BALANCE THE ACT

(KRIS)

♥ For most of us, life has become so crazy that it might be called a balancing act. Many of us are speeded-up, frenetic, nervous, anxious about time, and accomplishing tasks and doing things at an alarming rate. Even technology doesn't seem to help. Many of us have modern conveniences and time-saving gadgets, but few of us have enough time. This being the case, we must conclude that at least a portion of our inner turmoil must be coming from within ourselves and the way we are choosing to live.

It's important to ask ourselves whether we really want to go through the rest of our life out of control, flying by the seat of our pants, and treating life as if it were an emergency. Wouldn't it be nicer if we could calm down a little bit and regain our sense of perspective? One of the keys to regaining a feeling of peace and composure is creating at least some degree of balance in your life.

When we are out of balance, we often discover our health to be compromised, our family scrambling, and our relationships in turmoil. We end up always in a rush, forgetful, and extremely frustrated. Creating a sense of balance, however, seems to mitigate these sensations and replace them with feelings of peace and a sense that it's good to be alive.

A nice way to think of balance is to see your life as a pendulum that swings back and forth. Its ideal location is dead center—perfectly balanced.

As it swings too far to the left, you must make a few adjustments, enabling the pendulum to swing back to the right, and to find center again. The best monitor of how you are doing is the way you feel. Generally speaking, when you feel peaceful and contented, you're probably relatively close to center, on track, and making good choices. On the other hand, when you feel scattered or overwhelmed, you're probably off center, needing to make those adjustments.

Perhaps it's best to use a commonsense approach to strive for more balance. If at all possible, try to avoid extremes. Eighteen hours of work is obviously too much. Three hours of sleep isn't enough. You may not need excessive exercise every single day but, clearly, you do need some exercise on a regular basis. Again, think in terms of a balanced life. Make balanced decisions that support a healthy, happy lifestyle.

If you go on vacation and play hard for a week, you obviously may have to work longer hours to catch up when you return. That's okay; just don't overdo it. Conversely, if you are on a deadline that requires overtime, plan ahead. At the completion of the project, try to make it up by spending some extra time with your partner and family while spending a little less time working.

Also, stop rushing around. The feeling of the rush creates a great deal of anxiety for yourself and for the people around you, especially those you live with.

Years ago, we became aware of how out of balance and hurried our lives had become. It always seemed that we were running late, and as an infant and toddler Jazzy was always whining when we were getting ready to go somewhere. We realized that we were trying to do too much. We were cramming too many things into our days. We had to let a few things fall by the wayside in order to come back to balance. As soon as we began creating more balance, our lives became manageable once again.

Not too long ago, my best girlfriend and I were away for a weekend together. We overheard a conversation a woman was having about the experience she had had the day before. She was stuck in traffic for over two hours. She arrived at her destination and frantically parked the car. She was, of course, very late. To make matters worse, she had two screaming children in the backseat and couldn't get the stroller to unfold. At that moment, her cell phone rang. Just hearing the story made both of us nervous. Unfortunately, we had both been there before.

How does imbalance affect your relationship? Richard and I were once in a restaurant in Los Angeles. We looked over and saw two people who had obviously met for lunch, each on their cell phones, talking to other people. A little out of balance, wouldn't you say?

Choosing balance over chaos won't make your life perfect, but it will give you a much higher quality of life and deeper, more satisfying relationships. So, while we may never reach a perfect balance, any efforts we make in this regard will be well worth the effort.

99.

REMEMBER THE MAGIC

In a recent *Life* magazine article titled "The Science of Love," researchers explain that the "I can't get enough of you" (or "honeymoon" phase) in a relationship lasts from eighteen months to three years, after those first feelings of infatuation. So let's talk about a strategy that will help you recapture those feelings and remember the magic of falling in love. It's really quite simple: Keep the courtship going.

Make time in your busy schedules to be together. It's so easy to forget to take the time to acknowledge each other in the special ways we once did while we were dating. After all, life becomes saturated with careers and family responsibilities, while the intensity we once felt for each other often is replaced by feelings of normalcy and the routine of living. But if you dare to bring that spark back and step out of your routine, you'll be surprised at the result. Bring home flowers for no apparent reason, surprise him with a love letter at the office, write poetry for each other. Go on a walk, hand in hand. Do something! There are many simple ways to keep the courtship going that will help you to remember, cherish, and keep that magic alive.

After starting our family, nearly ten years ago, we found that we were lacking the quality time that we had always treasured. We could no longer go on our early-morning runs together, and even our ritual of drinking coffee was replaced with breast-feeding. While our budget was prohibitive, in those early years, we still found that in order to nurture our connection, we needed to make time for weekly scheduled "date nights."

Once you start your family, your relationship can definitely take the backseat, and if you're not careful, it can become lost in family life altogether. Although it seems there is always someone or something that needs tending to, or homework that needs to be completed, it's important that your life together remain a top priority.

It's well worth it, for example, to find a good babysitter or babysitting coop to care for your children a few hours each week, or month, so the two of you can enjoy each other without interruption. You will quickly remember why you like each other so much, and you will have more time to appreciate each other. While an evening is wonderful, a weekend away is even better. We have always made an attempt to take two or three mini-weekends away each year to rekindle that magic between us. If this is not plausible, any time you can arrange will help.

Take some time to reflect on those early days, weeks, and years together. Surprise your spouse with a ritual from your past and bring it to your present moments together. Do the things that you used to do; act out the love that you feel and you will reignite your connection and, what's more, you will remember the magic of falling in love.

100.

TREASURE EACH OTHER

♥ One of the most life-affirming, love-enriching messages you can send to your loved one is the message, "I treasure you." When someone knows they are treasured, they feel important and valued. This encourages them to treasure you back, to remain loyal and loving, and to feel as though your relationship is satisfying. When you get right down to it, letting someone know they are treasured is one of the greatest compliments you can give—and one of the best ways to say "I love you."

The best way to let someone know you treasure them is, you guessed it, to tell them. Be sure to let your partner know, frequently, what you like about them. Be specific. If you like their smile, their laugh, something they do, whatever, let them know. Don't make the mistake of assuming that your partner already knows what you like—they may not. You may not have told them for a long, long time.

One of the by-products of letting your partner know that you treasure them is that the positive aspects of your relationship are reinforced and strengthened. Your focus on your partner's positive traits, habits, and behavior keeps your attention on what's right with your relationship and what you enjoy about each other. It helps you dismiss the imperfections and keeps you from sweating the small stuff. In addition, when your partner is really clear about what you like about them, they are far more inclined to repeat the attitudes and behaviors that you find so appealing. For example, if you tell your partner, "I love the fact that you almost always remember to say thank you when I've gone out of my way to do something for you," he or she will almost certainly continue to do so. Your positive feedback reinforces and solidifies an already positive characteristic. If, on the other hand, you take this tendency for granted, and your partner doesn't even know you appreciate it, there would seem to be a much greater chance that it will fade away.

We have a close friend who is a psychologist specializing in, among other things, marriage counseling. She tells us it's very common for people to know what their partner doesn't like about them—but to have no idea of what they like or appreciate. No wonder they are in counseling! According to our friend, however, the slightest acknowledgment, and more focus on the positive instead of focusing exclusively on what could be or should be better, can turn a relationship around. Her conclusions seem consistent with our own observations.

One of the things that has always come naturally to the two of us is our willingness to share what we like with one another. For example, I've always loved the way Kris can be silly—and she knows I like it because I tell her. I also love how involved she is in the kids' lives, how talented she is in creating beauty wherever she goes, how easily she makes friends and makes people smile, and how incredibly forgiving she is. She, in turn, is quick to tell me she loves the way I'm willing to help around the house and how good I am with our kids. There are so many things we like about each other, and our willingness to share openly about our likes reinforces what is good in our relationship. I'd guess that with few exceptions, Kris and I have told each other at least one thing we like about each other every day since we've met.

Once, when we were having a rare conflict with one another, she said, "You know what, Richard? I really like the way you're willing to let go of things." You can imagine that we weren't mad at each other for very long.

Like most couples, we've been through many things in our time together—mostly good. However, one thing never changes: We really do treasure each other—and we hope you do too.